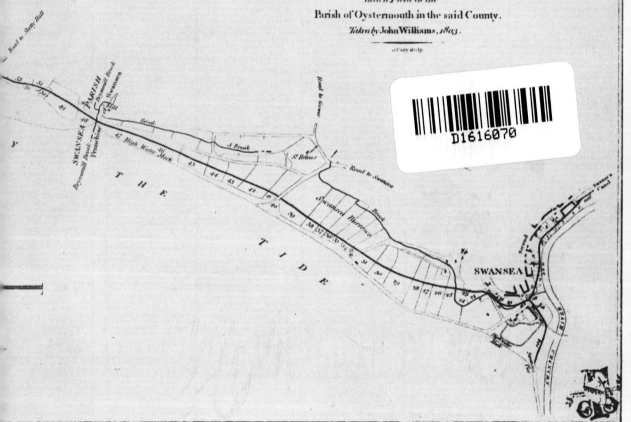

ROCK & ROLL TO PARADISE

The History of the Mumbles Railway

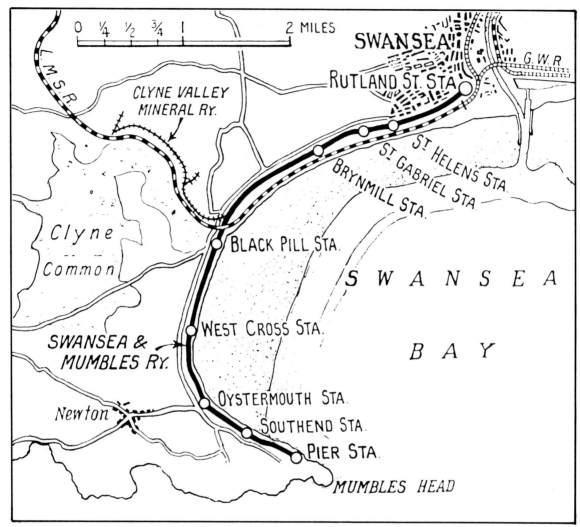

1   The Swansea and Mumbles Railway.

ROCK & ROLL TO PARADISE

The History of the Mumbles Railway

ROB GITTINS

GOMER PRESS

To Grace, Norman, David and Alison

First Impression - December 1982

ISBN 0 85088 638 4

Printed by
J. D. Lewis & Sons Ltd.
Llandysul, Dyfed.

CONTENTS

ACKNOWLEDGEMENTS

I would like to record my indebtedness to Wyn Thomas, formerly Programme Controller of ILR Swansea Sound, for initiating and directing the original radio documentary on which a large part of this book is based. His trust, courage and friendship have proved invaluable in both these projects and neither would have seen the light of day without him. I am also grateful for the generous help rendered by Tony Cottle, Chairman of the Mumbles Railway Society, Veronica Barrington, Secretary to the Mumbles Railway Society, Ron Lawson, Chairman of the Mumbles Railway Company, Jack Bartlett and Wynford Vaughan-Thomas. I would also like to acknowledge the varied and invaluable assistance of Finvola Davies, Dyfed Elis Gruffydd and Mary Deere. I am indebted to the pioneering research undertaken by Charles E. Lee into the early years of the Mumbles Railway, the help given by Professor Frank Llewellyn-Jones with respect to the early years of steam on the line and the research undertaken by the Light Railway Transport League into the circumstances surrounding the closure of the railway. Finally, I would like to thank all the above for their important respective roles in a campaign that may one day restore the Mumbles Railway back to Swansea.

PHOTOGRAPHIC ACKNOWLEDGEMENTS

The photographs in this book have been reproduced by kind permission of Tony Cottle; Veronica Barrington; Ron Lawson; R. E. James-Robertson; *South Wales Evening Post*; Swansea City Council; Mollie Phillips, O.B.E., J.P.; H. Buller; Alan Randall; Cynon Valley Borough Libraries; Leicestershire Museums, Art Galleries and Records Service. The line drawings were specially prepared for inclusion in the volume by Dorian Spencer Davies.

LIST OF ILLUSTRATIONS

Chapter 1

THE ESTABLISHMENT OF THE LINE

On 4 July 1804, the year Napoleon became Emperor, William Pitt was Prime Minister and George III was King of England; a small gathering assembled at a local inn in the Welsh seaside resort of Swansea. Twenty-one eminent local men crowded into an upper room of the town's Bush Inn to hear Sir John Morris, Baronet of Clasemont, read out a list of shareholders and welcome those same shareholders to the first meeting of a new company, the Oystermouth Railway or Tramroad Company. Those twenty-one men comprised its proprietors. Each had paid a minimum of £100 to launch its major undertaking, a complete new rail link from Swansea to the tiny village of Oystermouth. Each man present cheered their Chairman to the rafters as he opened the day's proceedings with a stirring call that the story of their enterprise and the name of Swansea's Oystermouth Railway should ring down through the ages, taking their names and the spirit of their purpose into the next century, the next century and each century after that! One year before the Battle of Trafalgar that may have sounded hopeful. But that small gathering was to launch one of the most significant events in history—the first passenger railway in the world.

Unknown even to its original promoters, that gathering was to launch an historic Rock and Roll to Paradise.

The last souvenir brochure commemorating the Mumbles Railway[1] comments that, at the beginning of the nineteenth century, Swansea was a 'gay resort of fashion'. The population of ten thousand people lived among acres of green fields, bordered by open country to one side and fringed on the other by the sandy

[1] South Wales Transport Company, *Swansea and Mumbles Railway: The Chain of Progress*, SWTC, 1960.

ANNO QUADRAGESIMO QUARTO

GEORGII III. REGIS.

Cap. 55.

An Act for making and maintaining a Railway or Tramroad from the Town of *Swansea*, into the Parish of *Oystermouth* in the County of *Glamorgan*. [29th *June* 1804.]

WHEREAS the making and maintaining of a Railway or Tramroad for the passage of Wagons and other Carriages, to communicate with the *Swansea* Canal near a certain Place called *The Brewery Bank*, within the Town of *Swansea* in the County of *Glamorgan* to, or near to a certain Field called *Castle Hill*, in the Parish of *Oystermouth* in the said County of *Glamorgan*; and also the making and maintaining of a Branch of such Railway or Tramroad, to communicate therewith, from a certain place near the *Mount* in the said Town of *Swansea*, in the County aforesaid, to, or nearly to, *Swansea* Pier; and likewise the making and maintaining of another Branch of such Railway or Tramroad, to communicate therewith, from a certain place near *Black Pill*, to or nearly to a certain place called *Ynys*, in the Parish of *Swansea* in the said County of *Glamorgan* will open a Communication with several extensive Limestone Quarries, Coal Mines, Iron Mines and other Mines, whereby the Carriage and Conveyance of Limestone, Coal, Iron Ore, and other Minerals and Commodities, will be greatly facilitated, and will materially assist the Agriculture of the Country throughout the Line and Neighbourhood thereof, and will in other respects be of great Public Utility; but the same cannot be effected without the Authority of Parliament. And whereas the several Persons herein-after named are willing and desirous at their own Expense, to make and maintain the said Railway or Tramroad, and the Branches thereof, as aforesaid: May it therefore please Your Majesty that it may be enacted; and be it enacted by the King's most Excellent Majetsy, by and with the Advice and Consent of the Lords Spiritual and Temporal, and Commons, in this present Parliament assembled, and by the Authority of the same, That the Most Noble *Henry Charles* Duke of *Beaufort*, the Burgesses of the Borough of *Swansea*, *Charles Collins*, *John Charles Collins*, *John Edmund*, *Benjamin French*, *Thomas Hobbes* Doctor of Physic, *Calvert Richard Jones*, *Edward King*, *John Landeg*, *Roger Landeg*, *Thomas Lockwood*, *Thomas Lott*, *Thomas Morgan*, *John Morris*, *John Morris* the younger, *Thomas Sylvester*, *William Vaughan*, and their several and respective Successors, Executors, Administrators, and Assigns, together with such Person and Persons as they shall nominate and appoint under their Hands and Seals, or the said Burgesses under their Common Seal, are and shall be united into a Company, for the better carrying on, making, completing, and maintaining the said intended Railway or Tramroad, with the Branches thereof as aforesaid, according to the Rules, Orders, and Directions, herein-after expressed and laid down, and shall for that Purpose be one Body Politic and Corporate, by the Name of *The Oystermouth Railway or Tramroad Company*.

2 Parliamentary Act incorporating the Oystermouth Railway.

1

dunes of Swansea Bay. Swansea was certainly an important seaport, but at the beginning of the last century it was more a market town of note than an industrial centre of significance. It was more renowned as a fashionable watering spa for the rich than as a trading area for the new professional classes. The old industries of salt and mineral mining still dominated the Swansea scene in 1800. The great copper works of the Vivians were not to appear for ten years, while the massive tin-plate, copper ore, lead and nickel industries that were to make Swansea one of the metallurgical centres of the world, were not to dominate the scene for another fifty years. But if the town's more genteel antecedents still predominated over the emerging industrial dynamism, the seeds of change were clearly discernible in the air. One contemporary author wrote at the start of the 1800s that Swansea,

. . . is a mixture of good and bad, of old streets and new, wide and narrow, pride and poverty, much show and little wealth. [2]

The contrasts captured in this description are indicative of the impending change and, in retrospect, can be seen as portents to the genteel resort that the new industrial age was hammering at its doors. It is against the back-cloth of this imminent transformation that the Oystermouth promoters put forward their plans for a new rail link for the town.

The main agent in the establishment of the railway, Sir John Morris of Clasemont, came from a family prominent in the emerging industrial enterprise. He mined copper, iron and coal, the latter principally at Ynys and Rhydydefaid collieries in the Clyne valley, and had pioneered the installation of a growing number of tramways in Welsh collieries. His interest in the machinery of the new age was confirmed when he was among the first to install Boulton and Watt steam engines into his collieries to pump water from underground

coal workings. [3] Morris himself was later to win personal fame for laying out the first 'garden city' in Wales, the township of Morriston, and in becoming one of the founders of the Royal Institution of South Wales. [4] The other members of the new Railway Board included the Duke of Beaufort, one of the largest landowners of the area on whose land much industrial development took place, and Edward Martin, a local colliery inspector and tramroad surveyor and one of the most prominent and progressive citizens of his age. All these men were to play an important part in the transition of Swansea from the decorous retreat to the 'ugly, lovely town' of Dylan Thomas' 1930s description. [5] They were all well aware that the new age of development and enterprise they wished to bring into being necessitated certain changes. One of the first they required was the establishment of an effective transport system for the town.

Initially the purpose of the new Oyster-mouth Railway was to transport limestone, coal and iron ore from the extensive quarries and mines in the Clyne valley and at Oystermouth. At that time no turnpike road followed the head of Swansea Bay; there was only an overland cart track, navigable at low tide, over the sandy beach to St. Helen's. The only alternative cargo transport was by sea, an equally hazardous and inefficient operation in which limestone and other minerals were loaded from the small quays at Mumbles onto a number of small boats and then transported across the bay to Swansea. The inadequacies of this service had been apparent for some time

[3] He shares this distinction with Samuel Homfray, the great ironmaster of Merthyr Tydfil. Homfray, as will be noted later, was to pursue his interest in steam engines to run the world's first steam rail locomotive in Merthyr in February, 1804.
[4] Morris founded the Royal Institution of South Wales in co-operation with two of the Swansea Dillwyns: Lewis Weston Dillwyn, F.R.S. and John Dillwyn Llewellyn, F.R.S. The Dillwyns and the Vivians were the two local families most intimately connected with the dawn of Swansea's industrial age.
[5] Dylan Thomas 'Reminiscences of Childhood', reprinted in Quite Early One Morning, London, 1967, p. 1.

[2] Source unknown.

and had led to various solutions being proposed, including one by Edward Martin himself for a *canal* link between Oystermouth and Swansea. The original plan of the railway clearly shows that, as late as 1803, the transport proposals for Swansea still included the option of *either* a canal *or* a railway, and the relative merits of these two schemes were being debated in the correspondence columns of Swansea's newspaper, *The Cambrian*, in the early part of 1804. That the choice fell eventually upon the railway must have been influenced in part by intense contemporary interest in the establishment of public railways elsewhere. The first public railway in Britain, the Surrey Iron Railway Company, had been incorporated by Act of Parliament just two years before the promotion of the Oystermouth proposals on 21 May 1801. The Carmarthenshire Railway or Tramroad Company had been incorporated on 3 June 1802, followed by the Sirhowy Tramroad on 26 June of that year. Rail transport, in fact, was fast becoming the standard bearer of the new industrial age. The promoters of the Oystermouth line were determined that they should not be left behind.

It is likely, however, that the early meetings and consultations between Sir John Morris and the rest of those original promoters were probably conducted in some secrecy as public opinion in Swansea seems to have been less than enthusiastic about their plans. The eventual publication of the Railway Bill provoked a heated correspondence in *The Cambrian* in the spring of 1804 but, fortunately for the Oystermouth promoters, the opposition appears to have dissipated itself in wranglings between those who opposed any development and those who proposed alternative systems for the link between Swansea and Mumbles. The Swansea Corporation for their part accepted proposals for constructing *either* a canal *or* a railway from Swansea to Oystermouth and the battle was thus taken to the House of Commons where the united resolve of the railway promoters was indeed to prove to greater effect. In February, 1804, the Railway Bill was introduced and on 22 June 1804, *The Cambrian* informed its readers that,

> . . . the Bill for making a Railway or Tramroad from this town to Oystermouth has passed both Houses of Parliament.

Parliament had thus acquiesced to the construction of the railway, but had declined to include any proposals for a canal. Seven days later this was confirmed when the 'Act for making and maintaining a Railway or Tramroad from the town of Swansea into the Parish of Oystermouth' received Royal Assent and became law.

The preamble to the Bill gave a detailed account of the route Swansea's new railway would take. It would,

> . . . communicate with the Swansea canal near a certain place called the Brewery Bank within the town of Swansea in the County of Glamorgan to, or near to, a certain field called Castle Hill in the Parish of Oystermouth . . .

An additional stretch of line would,

> . . . communicate therewith from a certain place called the Mount in the said town of Swansea in the County aforesaid to, or nearly to, the Swansea Pier . . .

Whilst a third section would,

> . . . communicate therewith from a certain place near Blackpill to, or nearly to, a certain place called Ynys in the Parish of Swansea in the said County of Glamorgan.

Its stated purpose was to,

> . . . open up a communication with several extensive limestone quarries, local mines, iron mines and other mines, whereby the carriage and conveyance of limestone, coal, iron-ore and other minerals and commodities will be greatly facilitated and will materially assist the agriculture of the country throughout the line and neighbourhood thereof, and will in other respects be of great public utility.

Following the publication of this Bill matters moved quickly. Within a week that first general assembly of the Railway Company was held on 4 July at the Bush Inn. A Committee of Management was elected—with Sir John Morris in the chair—which held their first meeting five days later.[6] This meeting put the new line's construction plans into immediate effect, accepting a proposal that Messrs Homfray, Tappendens and Birch of Abernant Iron-Works Merthyr Tydfil, be approved to supply iron tram-plates delivered at the Swansea Quay for the sum of £7 a ton and further ordering that a 'call of £5 per cent from the subscribers to and proprietors of this undertaking be made and paid to the hands of the Treasurer at the Glamorgan and Swansea Bank on or before the sixth day of August next'. With the preliminaries thus completed in just twelve days, construction of the Railway was planned to start in the autumn of 1804.

According to the 'Mumbles Railway Centenary Souvenir of 1904' the original permanent way of the railway consisted of 3 ft. lengths of angle iron; the typical cast-iron tram plates of the period. These were attached onto blocks of granite by dog spikes, and with these rails possessing a projecting flange the wheels of the carriages themselves did not require flanges. This system was used extensively throughout South Wales in the early years of the nineteenth century and, as Charles Lee notes, Parliament clearly expected the Oystermouth line to use a similar system as the Act of 1804 not only authorised a Railway or Tramroad, but also included the following provision,[7]

And it be further enacted that wherever the said intended Railway or Tramroad shall cross any private or public way or road, the plates of the said Railway or Tramroad shall be made for the wheels of the carriages used thereon to run in a groove and from the highest part of the plates the sides each way shall be made aslant in such a way as that carriages of all kinds may easily pass over the same.

The actual laying of the track began in September, 1805, when £2,794/0/6d was credited to Messrs Homfray, Tappendens and Birch for their supply of tram plates and castings, and it was not long before the inhabitants of Swansea began to witness its presence. The first section of line was laid at the Brewery Bank near the bottom of the Cwm, adjacent to the old Swansea canal. From there a section was laid along the Strand to the Royal Institution with one branch line running off onto land later called Bath Lane. This section in fact required the demolition of the town's ancient Mount which was built on Corporation land between Somerset Place and opposite the Somerset Buildings, and entailed also the levelling of its ground. The next stretch of line continued across the Burrows to Bond Street and then along the sandhills themselves between Swansea and Oystermouth. It passed along the beach to Gorse Lane and then between the sandbanks and Singleton Park to Blackpill. The line then went back along the beach to Oystermouth while another branch line led off this stretch of track, following the Clyne valley to a terminus at Ynys. At Oystermouth the line went back on the road to connect to the village's limestone quarries.[8] Before this con-

[6] This Committee of Management comprised Sir John Morris, Thomas Lockwood, John Morris jnr., Thomas Lott, Edward Martin, Benjamin French, the Portreeve of Swansea and Dr. Thomas Hobbes.

[7] Charles E. Lee, *The First Passenger Railway*, Oakwood Press, South Godstone, Surrey, 1942, reprinted as *The Swansea and Mumbles Railway*, 1954, 1977, p. 29.

[8] This system was inspected by two Prussian engineers in 1827 who provide what is now the most detailed surviving description of the line. Their report states that the line was about '7 English miles long with a gauge of 47 ins.' It reported that the track was almost entirely level as it followed the coastline around the bay. Of the rails themselves, each was 35 ins. long and 3½ ins. wide without the flange. Their thickness was measured at 1½ ins., although the end of the rails tapered to just ⅝ ins. The flange was measured at 2½ ins. high, ⅓ ins. thick at the top and ½ ins. thick at the bottom. cf. *The Swansea and Mumbles Railway*, op.cit., p. 30.

struction was complete, another general assembly of the proprietors was held at the Guildhall, Swansea, on 6 January 1806 where special 'bye-laws and orders' were approved and ordered to be published, clearly in anticipation of the early opening of the line to traffic. The Oystermouth promoters, in fact, had to wait another three months for that day but in April, 1806, the first goods traffic finally passed over their new track.

The Oystermouth Railway immediately began to fulfil its original and stated purpose of transporting minerals; iron ore, coal and limestone from Oystermouth and the Clyne valley to Swansea. The local business community were circulated with the Railway Company's schedule for that service,

Tonnage rates

For all Iron, Goods, Wares and Merchandise except as below	4d per ton per mile
For all Iron Castings	3d per ton per mile
For all Pig Iron	2½d per ton per mile
For all Iron-stone, Coloured Iron-ore, Rottenstone, Coals, Culm, Stone-coal, Coke, Cinders, Charcoal, Timber, Stones, Tiles, Bricks and Clay.	1½d per ton per mile

Fractions of a mile to be paid for as the Quarters therein of a ton, for a quarter of a mile as a whole ton.

The Company also have the power of charging according to their discretion for parcels not exceeding five hundredweight.

But the *major* point of interest in those first twelve months was *not* to be the sight of

3 No photographs exist of the mineral wagons on the Oystermouth Railroad, but they are likely to have been similar to the above. The photograph is of the Penderyn tramway in the Cynon Valley and dates from the nineteenth century.

mineral traffic using the new line. The major point of interest was rather the prospect of a unique and novel proposition mooted by one of the railway's original promoters just ten months after the line's opening.

This promoter was one Benjamin French, 'Gentleman of Swansea' whose name appears among the original list of proprietors and who was a member of the original Committee of Management. His proposition to the Railway Company was that he should institute a very different sort of service on the new Oystermouth line; that he be granted permission to 'run a wagon or wagons on the Tramroad for one year from 25th March next, for the conveyance of *passengers*'.[9] His proposal was accepted by a meeting of the Committee of the Company of Proprietors on 16 February 1807, who ordered that 'two check gates be erected on the Tramroad, one at the south opening into the Brewery Yard and the other near Hughes Forge'.[10] Just one month later, Benjamin French ran his first passenger carriage on the Oystermouth line.

The early promoters, passengers and the spectators who watched, probably in some amusement, the odd contraption grinding noisily along the tram rails were not to know that they were witnessing an outstanding event in the history of rail transport. They were not to know that, by virtue of that single journey, Benjamin French had succeeded in engraving the name of Swansea's Oystermouth Railway on the history books for ever. For on 25 March 1807, on the Oystermouth line, Benjamin French made the *first* passenger journey by rail anywhere in the world. By so doing, he had unwittingly inaugurated the whole era of passenger travel by rail.

Such a phenomenon did not pass without comment. The earliest surviving reference to the new passenger service appeared in 1809 when Elisabeth Isabella Spence published her *Summer Excursions through parts of Oxfordshire, Gloucestershire, Warwickshire, Staffordshire, Herefordshire, Derbyshire and South Wales*. This volume, consisting of letters from the much-travelled author to the Dowager Countess of Winterton, spoke warmly of the new railway,

> I have never spent an afternoon with more delight than the former one in exploring the romantic scenery at Oystermouth. I was conveyed there in a carriage of singular construction built for the conveniency of parties who go hence to Oystermouth to spend the day. This car contains twelve persons and is constructed chiefly of iron, its four wheels run on an iron railway by the aid of one horse, and the whole carriage is an easy and light vehicle.[11]

This new service seems to have become well established by the time Nicholas Carlisle published his *Topographical Dictionary of Wales* in 1811,

> A Railway has been carried within the last three years from Swansea to the Mumbles along the seashore; by which Coals and Manure are brought down and Limestone is taken back. A car, upon Tram wheels and carrying about 16 or 18 persons, goes and returns twice every day, during the summer, down to the Mumbles; each passenger paying a shilling fare; it is convenient for Sea-faring people and others, and the Proprietor amply repays himself; who has permission from the Rail-road company to run this car, upon paying a small sum annually.

The advantages of the new line were recorded in a local publication, *A Description of Swansea and Its Environs*, printed and sold by David Jenkins of Castle Street, Swansea, in 1813,

---

[9] Quoted in the account and minute books of the Oystermouth Railway or Tramroad Company, in the possession of Mr. E. A. Watkins, formerly secretary of the Swansea and Mumbles Railway Company. (My emphasis appears in the quotation).

[10] Ibid.

[11] This is taken from Letter No. XIV, dated Swansea, 3 August 1808.

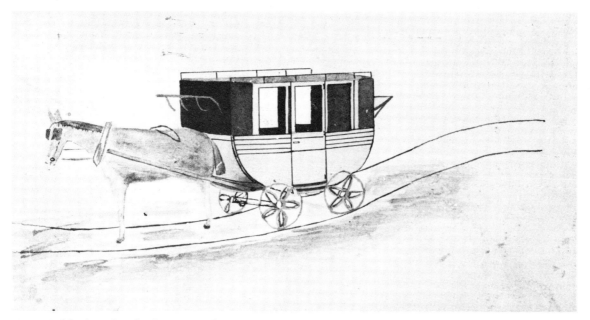

4 J. Ashford's sketch depicting the passenger carriage on the Oystermouth Railway. Dated 1819.

. . . many pleasant parties are formed by this conveyance and by taking the first that goes down in the morning and returning with the latest in the evening, much of the beautiful scenery may be seen within a few miles for the small expence of two shillings each person.

These advantages were still being enjoyed in 1821 when a traveller from Newbury, identified in his journal only by his initials W.M.L., set off for the Mumbles on the Oystermouth train. The gentleman,

. . . set off at four o'clock in the afternoon in the car for the Mumbles with a very pleasant companion . . . We started an hour later than we ought as the man was waiting for some ladies who had taken places to go with us. The car is intended to carry sixteen persons and runs on a railway drawn by one horse. The distance is five miles from Swansea turnpike to the Mumbles. We had ten persons with us and . . . among the ladies were two very pretty delicate girls

apparently only visitors for their health to Swansea. I was much pleased with my ride being all along the sands on the railway before mentioned, the scenery grand particularly Oystermouth Castle and the Bay of Swansea. [12]

The first passenger carriages were, apparently, adaptations of the mineral wagons used on the tramroad. The two surviving pictures from this period, particularly J. Ashford's sketch of 1819, certainly lend support to this view and the novelty of the ride must thus have been at the expense of some degree of comfort. Indeed, one of the only surviving notes of complaint about the new passenger service, recorded by Richard Ayton in *A Voyage Around Great Britain Undertaken in 1813*, made just that point,

We made an excursion to Oystermouth, a

[12] I am indebted to Thomas Lloyd of Court Henry, Dryslwyn, for drawing my attention to this reference. The private journal in which this reference appears is in Mr. Lloyd's possession.

village near the western extremity of Swansea Bay in a tram car, a singular kind of vehicle established for the accommodation of visitors to this place. It is a very long carriage, supported on four low iron wheels, carries sixteen persons, exclusive of the driver, is drawn by one horse and rolls along over an iron rail-road, at the rate of five miles an hour, and with the noise of twenty sledge hammers in full play. The passage is only four miles, but it is quite sufficient to make one reel from the car at the journey's end in a state of dizziness and confusion of the senses that it is well if he recovers in a week.

And the new rail service also offended the poet Walter Savage Landor, though his objections were aesthetic rather than practical,

How beautiful was the seashore covered with low roses, yellow snapdragons and thousands of other plants. That streak of black along the most beautiful coast in the universe will never succeed in rendering me indifferent to Swansea. Two years afterwards the detestable tram road was made along it. Besides before this, thousands of small vessels covered the bay laden with lime and whatever else is now carried in those train wagons.

But it seems that acclamation outweighed criticism, because one year after his first passenger carriage trundled along the Oystermouth track, Benjamin French, together with two other promoters, offered the Railway Company an *increased* sum for the renewal of the passenger lease. Passenger traffic, it appears, was a profitable venture.

Though 1807 was to be an outstanding year in the history of the new railway, not all the ideas put forward in that pioneering year worked quite so well. A particularly novel 'experiment', undertaken on the Oystermouth line a mere month after the introduction of the passenger service, was reported in *The Cambrian* on 18 April 1807,

5 Mock-up of sail train run experimentally on the Oystermouth Railway in 1807. The photograph dates from 1865.

An experiment of a novel kind was carried out on the Oystermouth tramroad yesterday to ascertain the practicability of a carriage proceeding to the Mumbles without horse, by the aid of wind alone. Some jolly sons of Neptune rigged a wagon with a long sail and the wind blowing strong and as fair as could be wished set off from our quay and after clearing the houses dropped anchor at the end of the tramroad in less than three quarters of an hour, having come a distance of about 4½ miles.

This method of traction was *abandoned* after the one experimental journey, horses perhaps being deemed less subject to the vagaries of wind currents!

A directors' meeting held on 19 February 1808, one year after the establishment of the passenger service, reviewed the progress of the Oystermouth line. It should, by rights, have been a happy affair. The new line had been constructed and established, the mineral wagons had duly commenced their service and, in addition, a passenger service had been instituted to complement the line's original function. So—a good start for those directors? Sadly, it was not to prove good enough.

In the meeting of 19 February 1808 the attention of the Management Committee was diverted *away* from the excitement and innovation that accompanied the opening of the railway and from the pioneering nature of the enterprise and fixed, very firmly, on its *cost*. The directors disclosed two disturbing items of information to the shareholders; that the sum of £9,394/2/0d had been spent from 1804 to 1808 in building the Oystermouth line, and that in the previous full year from 1 January to 31 December, 1807, only £160 had been received in tolls. Examination of the original register of shareholders reveals that of the 80 shares of £100 which the Company was authorised by its Act of Incorporation to issue, 72 had been subscribed for and paid, thus raising a total of £7,200 of capital. The original cost of construction thus far exceeded raised share capital and the small remuneration in the form of tolls contributed little to balance the net deficit of £2,194.

These financial circumstances were such that the Railway Company was forced to borrow £1,500 on the security of three 'assignments of tolls by way of mortgage' from four mortgagees, William Fendell, Charles Evans, James Jelf and William Stroud on 6 July 1808. Interest was fixed at 5 per cent per annum. Fortified by this infusion of cash the rail service continued, but seven years later found itself in trouble again. In 1815 the Railway Company defaulted on its mortgage repayments and the mortgagees entered into possession of the line. The last shareholders meeting in this period took place on 1 April 1816, after which the Railway Company was dispossessed of its property.

But *why* should the Railway Company have been dispossessed of its property? Why, with the spirit, enterprise and enthusiasm that launched the railway should it have found itself in such disastrous financial straits? No *one* cause is to blame but several factors can be identified.

In the first instance, the nature of the traffic carried on the line was open to abuse. There are indications that traffic consisted almost exclusively of that offered by the shareholders themselves, and evidence also suggests that this was paid for on the basis of agreed charges rather than by established tolls—charges likely to have been considerably less than those authorised by the Company's schedule of 1806. The original (and subsequent) arrangements between Benjamin French and the Railway Company illustrate the somewhat lax financial arrangements that were in operation. The proposal that the Committee of the Company of Proprietors accepted on 26 February 1808, for example, stated that 'Messrs French, Rose and Llewellyn proposed to run a wagon or wagons on the road for the conveyance of passengers from Lady Day next for a year' and that they would 'pay £25 *in lieu of tolls*' for that privilege.[13] That the Company's tolls were set aside in Mr French's case appears to have been typical of the Company's practice when dealing with traffic offered by other shareholders too.

It must also be said that this mismanagement was compounded by a high degree of ill-fortune. The original location of the railway, so close to the foreshore, resulted inevitably in periodic flooding of the track which necessitated not only costly repairs and re-levelling, but also on occasions the complete construction of new stretches of line further inland. Both factors exacerbated the instability of an already under-capitalised venture.

Thus a new management took over in 1816 and continued to offer a cargo and passenger service on the Oystermouth line. It was not, however, *completely* new for the management retained the services of one of the most promi-

[13] My emphasis.

9

nent of the original promoters, Sir John Morris, who had negotiated the first loan with the mortgagees in 1808. In his new capacity Sir John Morris seems now to have displayed all the astute qualities that brought the railway into existence, for in 1819 he became one of the mortgagees in possession of the line while in 1823 an assignment and transfer was made from the estates of the other two mortgagees to Morris. Thus seven years after being dispossessed of his line, Morris was once more in effective control of the Oystermouth Railway! But the management of the line mattered less than its performance and, sadly, its continuation from 1816 should not be taken as evidence that the new management was succeeding where its previous directors had failed. Traffic declined steadily throughout this period and a significant reference in

Brewster's *Edinburgh Encyclopaedia* of 1824 noted,

> . . . at Oystermouth a stage coach plies daily with passengers *which appear to be its chief trade.*[14]

It seems from this reference that the line was now not even fulfilling its original function of transporting mineral traffic and, despite the continued presence of Sir John Morris on the board of the Company, the line's commercial receipts appeared to have become dangerously dependent on those minor receipts from contractors who maintained the passenger traffic. These financial problems were once more exacerbated by natural misfortune, as in 1824 severe flooding again washed away a large

[14] My emphasis.

6   Original Oystermouth terminus before extension of line to Pier.

section of track resulting in extensive—and expensive—resiting work.

Thus eight years on from the collapse of the old company, the new outfit found itself, for much the same reasons, faring little better. These problems were compounded in 1826 when a new turnpike road was constructed between Swansea and Oystermouth. Mathews' *Swansea Directory 1830-1* described this new link as,

> . . . an excellent road . . . a finer piece is not to be found in the Principality.

Unfortunately for the railway, many of its passengers agreed with this assessment. One year prior to the opening of the turnpike road a general assembly of the Railway Company, again held in the Bush Inn, had heard a statement read by Sir John Morris of the tolls and dues received by the railway from 1819 to 1824. The hopelessness of the railway's financial position and looming competition from the new road now sounded the death knell for his enterprise. The Oystermouth Railway struggled on for one more year, as it had struggled on for so many, but the writing was now clearly on the wall In 1827, 23 years after its inception, the Oystermouth Railway found itself unable to continue operation and closed to passenger traffic.

Chapter 2

STEAM!

The closure of the Oystermouth Railway in 1827 confirmed the trend to road transport in the area of Swansea and the Mumbles. With the withdrawal of the rail service proprietors of horse-drawn coaches soon established a passenger service on the new highway, especially during the busy summer months. This service, according to the *Swansea Guide of 1851*, was frequent and convenient, running from Rees', the Horse and Groom and College Street twice a day and from Barters', the Rutland Arms and the Bush Inn three times a day. In addition, a service ran from the Railway Booking Office in Wind Street at frequent intervals during the day. Mineral traffic also utilised the new road link as did the postal service from Mumbles along the bay. The Pilot Post coach now rattled along the Mumbles road twice daily, at ten in the morning and three in the afternoon. Alongside these new carriages the Oystermouth Railway lay virtually derelict accommodating only a sporadic cargo of goods traffic. Rail transport in the Mumbles had faded almost as quickly as it had arrived, and it seemed as if the dawn of one age of transport had been just as quickly eclipsed by another.

Though the railway had fallen into disuse, the Railway Company was still in existence. But it was hardly an active existence and there is no record of any transactions for fourteen years after the line closed in 1827. Throughout this time the ageing Sir John Morris was still in charge of the Oystermouth Railway although the Company's lack of activity since 1827 made it highly unlikely that he would now be able to revive the railway he had established and struggled so hard to keep running earlier in the century. Additional evidence supporting this view was provided in 1840 when Company records reveal that he transferred

ten of his shares—numbers 52 to 61 inclusive —to be held in trust, 'to and for the sole use and benefit of George Byng Morris'.

These shares possessed a nominal value of £1000 and were held in trust for Morris by William Thomas, clerk to the Oystermouth Railway. This transfer marked the end of Sir John Morris' long association with the Oystermouth line, though the transfer of ten shares to George Byng Morris must have represented a hope on his part that a Morris might yet again prove the salvation of the line. Whatever his motives, it proved to be a fortuitous transfer.

It is important to note that this share transfer also included a secondary indenture whereby Sir John Morris transferred his mortgage and 'arrears of interest', again to be held in trust for George Byng Morris. This did not mean that the younger Morris immediately assumed ownership of the Oystermouth line. The mortgage seems to have remained in the possession of one of the executors, John James, probably as security on the original loan. On James' death in 1846, letters of administration were granted to one Robert Terry on 18 April who, by an indenture of 12 June 1847, finally and formally transferred the mortgage to George Byng Morris. This tortuous financial manoeuvering, however, was later dismissed by Morris when he said that he had in 1840,

> . . . entered into the actual possession of the said Oystermouth Railway and the undertaking land and works thereof . . . and has remained in the undisturbed possession of the same and worked and carried on the same at his own expense and received the tolls rents issues and profits thereof for his own use ever since the date of the last-mentioned indenture (11 January 1840) without giving any principal or interest and

he is now the absolute owner of the said Oystermouth Railway and the undertaking land and works thereof.

The truth or otherwise of this pleading now matters less than the impression it sought to create. For it was clear, from the date of the original share transfer, that George Byng Morris had seen himself very firmly in the role of absolute proprietor; a view later confirmed by the fact that from 1847 he made no essential formal entries in the Company's List of Proprietors—a prerequisite to normal corporate existence. But the fact that Morris assumed the role of absolute proprietor was at least consistent with the task he had set himself—to revive singlehandedly the old Oystermouth line.

Although road transport dominated the means of communication between Swansea and Oystermouth, Morris' first attempt at reviving the Oystermouth Railway came as part of a *larger* scheme to extend the original line along the Clyne valley through Dunvant and Llew to join the Llanelly Railway at Pontarddulais. To promote this undertaking, Morris registered a new company, the Swansea Docks and Mineral Vallies Company (*sic*) in 1855. This Company was formed in association with George Grant Francis who was later to be instrumental in the promotion of Swansea's *street* tramway system. In the same year part of the derelict Oystermouth track was relaid and a section of line reopened to transport coal from Rhydydefaid colliery in the Clyne valley to Swansea.[1] This colliery was under the control of a London company which undertook to transport the coal from the pit head to Ynys from where Morris transported it to the Strand. From 1855 onwards, Morris restored and renovated the original Oystermouth line section by section and though his scheme for a larger transport

network based on that line were not to materialise, his efforts did not go completely unrewarded. Ignoring the established road services on the Mumbles highway, Morris, on 27 July 1860, reopened the passenger service on the Oystermouth Railway from Swansea's Royal Institution to Blackpill.

At this stage it is useful to enquire *why* it should have been such an ambition of Morris' to reopen the Oystermouth line? Was it simply a desire to perpetuate what had already become a renowned local tradition? Or was it a determination to revive a viable business undertaking that, perhaps through lack of effective direction, had never been properly exploited? The weight of evidence now seems to favour the latter. It is now clear that Morris set his plans to revive the Oystermouth Railway into motion not on the basis of some individual whim, but to exploit an exciting and, potentially, highly lucrative contemporary phenomenon. It is now clear that Morris revived the Oystermouth Railway in order that it might participate in the approaching and burgeoning era of *steam*.

It may come as a surprise to learn that it was the original promoters of the Oystermouth line who first conceived the idea of a steam railway, but strong evidence supporting this view is contained in a critical passage in the line's original Act of Incorporation of 1804. This states that the 'haling and drawing of waggons and other carriages' on the new Oystermouth Railway was to be achieved by 'men, by horses, *or otherwise*'.[2] It was probably interpreted at the time as just a matter of legal phraseology allowing, for example, the substitution of horses by mules. However, a closer examination of the contemporary situation suggests that the inclusion of the phrase 'or otherwise' was intended to cover the introduction of a very different type of traction on the Oystermouth line.

At the time the Oystermouth Bill was submitted to Parliament in 1804, the engineer Richard Trevithick was running his historic

---

[1] Morris adopted the standard gauge track of 4 ft 8½ ins and used flat bottomed edge rails weighing 28 lbs to the yard. These rails were attached by spikes to transverse wooden sleepers. This system of standard gauge track was used widely on other Welsh mainline railways at this time.

[2] My emphasis.

7   Single-decked horse-drawn coach on the Oystermouth Railway, 1860s.

steam locomotion trials on Samuel Homfray's Penydarren tramroad at Merthyr Tydfil. These were to be the first successful steam locomotion trials in Britain with Trevithick's engine hauling a load of ten tons of iron and some 70 men along a 9 mile length of track. At least one of the original promoters of the Oystermouth line had publicised his strong support of Trevithick's new steam vehicles and his desire to see steam traction providing the motive power on the Oystermouth line. In a letter to *The Cambrian* on 10 March 1804, Edward Martin wrote,

> It had always appeared to me that the whole line from Oystermouth to Swansea should either be by a canal or Tramroad and therefore powers (as is well known) are intended

to be taken to carry either into effect as may be most expedient; and I have no hesitation in declaring that if Mr Trevithick's very ingenious machine is brought to perfection which some persons are confident it will be and which from the very liberal patronage it has received from Mr Homfray of Penydarren there is every reason to hope for, that is of driving waggons on a Tramroad at a cheaper rate by 50 per cent than it can now be done by horses, that it will be most advantageous to the proprietors and the public to substitute an entire tram road instead of a canal.

This letter appeared only a month after a report of Trevithick's steam locomotive

8 Double-decked horse-drawn coach on the Oystermouth Railway, 1860s.

experiment was carried in the 25 February issue of the same newspaper,

Yesterday the long expected trial of Mr Trevithick's new-invented steam engine for which he has obtained His Majesty's letters patent, to draw and work carriages of all descriptions on various kinds of roads, as well as for a number of other purposes, to which its power may be usefully applied, took place near this town and was found to perform with admiration, all that was expected from it by its warmest advocates. In the present instance, the novel application of steam, by means of this truly valuable machine was made use of to convey along the Tramroad ten tons long weight of bar-iron from Pendarren (sic) Ironworks, to the place where it joins the Glamorganshire Canal, upwards of nine miles distance; and it is necessary to observe, that the weight of the load was soon increased from ten to fifteen tons, by about seventy persons riding on the Trams who drawn thither (as well as many hundreds of others) by invincible curiosity, were eager to ride at the expense of this first display of the patentee's abilities in this country. To those who are not acquainted with the exact principle of this new engine, it may not be improper to observe, that it differs from all others yet brought before the public, by disclaiming the use of condensing water, and discharges its steam into the open air or applies it to the heating of fluid, as convenience may require. The expense of taking engines on this principle does not exceed one half if any on the most improved plans made use of before this appeared; it takes much less coal to work it, and it is only necessary to supply a small quantity of water for the purpose of creating the steam, which is a most essential matter. It performed on the journey without feeding the boiler or using any water and will travel with ease at five miles an hour. It is not doubted but that the number of horses in the kingdom will be very considerably reduced, and the machine in the hands of the present proprietors, will be made use of in a thousand instances never yet thought of for an engine.

The strong local interest in Trevithick's experiment was demonstrated by the appearance of another report in *The Cambrian* of 9 March 1804, the day before Edward Martin's letter was published,

An experiment was last tried at Llanelly by Mr Henry Vivian, engineer to Mr Trevithick's patent engines, by working the same with stone coal which predicts an acquisition to the proprietors of those works hitherto unexpected. This experiment, we understand, has been unsuccessfully tried under boilers constructed in the ordinary way.

The engine performs operation for six hours with the greatest exactness, consuming 1 cwt. 3 qrs of coal during that time, and executing the duty of four horses; nor did the fire require to be disturbed to maintain its heat, as requisite in other types of coal. We have therefore every reason to suppose the success of this experiment arises from the formation of the fireplace, which materially differs from any we have seen, and we trust that this intelligence will prove of some moment to those gentlemen who possess such property particularly in inland situations. We shall enlarge on this interesting subject when a further opportunity offers.

These articles—others appeared on 24 February and 12 May—lend strong support to the view that the Oystermouth promoters were, at the very least, fully appraised of the latest developments in steam traction. But what is also clear is that many of those same promoters were actually connected in various ways with the pioneers of steam traction. It's already been seen that many of the great families of Swansea were represented among the shareholders of the Oystermouth Railway and, among these families, the Vivians had close links with the new steam experiments through Henry Vivian, engineer to Trevithick who operated at Llanelli. Trevithick himself had arrived at Homfray's Ironworks in Merthyr Tydfil from Coalbrookdale where Sir John Morris, Chairman of the Oystermouth Railway, had extensive commercial and business interests, and the activities of Homfray himself, Trevithick's financial backer, were also intimately connected with the business life of Swansea and Mumbles. His company's advertisements appeared regularly in *The Cambrian*,

Messrs Homfray, Tappendens and Birch having established an iron-works at Abernant near Merthyr-Tidvil, Glamorganshire, beg to inform the public that they are now prepared to cast and fit-up STEAM ENGINES upon Mr Trevithick's and Boulton and Watt's plan, or ENGINES of any description according to order. Likewise all sorts of CASTINGS for COLLIERIES, COPPER or MINE-WORKS.

Mr. James Birch, the managing partner, (being an experimental engineer) flatters himself that, from the situations of the concern, he shall be able to execute orders for engines and castings of every description, in as good a manner and upon reasonable terms on any work in the Principality taking care of use Metal of a quality according to the work the Casting is to perform.

PRESENT PRICES
e.g.   Cylinders bored
       Piston and Bottoms turned
       Working Barrels   £28 per ton

All bored and turned goods
Rails and Dram-plates   9 ditto
Abernant Iron-Works, March 1st, 1804

This advertisement was dated 1 March 1804, precisely the time that the proposals to establish the Oystermouth Railway were being introduced before Parliament. It will also be recalled that, later that year, the Oystermouth Railway Company ordered tram plates and castings from Homfray's Ironworks at Abernant in order to begin construction of the Oystermouth line. These close links support the view that the careful phrasing of the original Act was intended to cover the introduction of steam traction once, as Edward Martin noted, Mr Trevithick's 'ingenious machine' had been brought to perfection. It is now a matter of record that steam traction could not be brought to perfection in 1804.[3] But it *could* some fifty years later.

Initially, when the Oystermouth Railway reopened in 1860 the horse-drawn traction, abandoned in 1827, was reintroduced. The restored service first ran from the Royal Institution to Blackpill although later that year the remainder of the main line was relaid and, from 10 November 1860, the full service from Swansea to Oystermouth once more operated. Despite the rival road service, the revived railway seems to have become an immediate success and indeed, as Norman L. Thomas notes,[4] even prompted the revival of other attractions of the area which had also fallen into disuse. One such attraction was reported in *The Cambrian* later that year,

Some of our sporting readers will be glad to find that the above races are again revived,

and are to take place on 4 August next. From the very attractive programme got up by the indefatigable exertions of Mr Abel Vivian of the 'Red Lion Inn', Blackpill, a few hours good sport is anticipated. Since the opening of the Oystermouth Railroad for passenger traffic great facilities will be afforded to parties, as there will be trains running at intervals of half-an-hour on that day.[5]

To begin with Morris ran *five* weekday trains each way with an extra train on Sundays. For the next few months the line appears to have attracted as much attention as the original service in 1807; and this newly restored popularity seemed well set to reward Morris' faith. But it was an undertaking that could not now stand still and having reopened the line the enterprising Mr Morris now initiated steps to ascertain the practicability of replacing the horse-drawn carriages with a more efficient method of mechanical traction. Indeed, Morris would have been guilty of an uncharacteristic lapse of foresight had he not. For at the time Morris reopened the passenger service on the Oystermouth line, other interested bodies in Swansea were contemplating just that step.

Less than twelve months after the reopening of the railway, Morris felt the first hot breath of competition following him closely down the line. During the 1860s there was intense interest in the establishment of passenger railways throughout South Wales and the lucrative Oystermouth route would certainly have appeared as one of the more attractive lines of the area. Various organisations petitioned to take advantage of the route despite the presence of Morris' revived line, and less than a year after its revival one company was successful. Vigorous lobbying in Parliament by the Llanelly Railway and Dock Company who argued that the Oystermouth route would benefit from a measure of competition, led to Parliament's acquiescence. Consequently, the Llanelly Railway (New Lines) Act of 1 August 1861, authorised con-

---

[3] This was less to do with any technical deficiencies in Trevithick's engines, however, than lack of financial backing for their operation. Sadly Trevithick was not able to exploit fully his pioneering work in steam rail locomotion and despite further trials in Merthyr Tydfil and London, the establishment of a regular steam locomotion service had to be left to 'Locomotion' of the Stockton and Darlington Railway in 1825.

[4] Norman L. Thomas, *The Mumbles: Past and Present*, UBS, Swansea 1978, p. 79.

[5] *The Cambrian*, 27 July 1860.

9 Close view of double-decked horse-drawn coach on the Oystermouth Railway, 1865.

struction of a new railway between the Oystermouth Railway and the sea which would parallel the Oystermouth line from Swansea to near Blackpill at which point it would cross over the Oystermouth line by way of a bridge and continue up the Clyne valley to Killay and Gowerton. Worse was to follow. This Act also indicated that, in places along the coast, the new railway would actually occupy the same track as the Oystermouth Railway and thereby necessitate its diversion inland. The intended method of traction for the new railway was to be *steam*.

Not unnaturally, friction immediately arose between the existing operators and the new Llanelly Railway Company, and heightened in June 1863 when Watson and Company, contractors for the Llanelly Railway, took possession of the relevant stretches of land alongside the Oystermouth Railway and began construction of the line. To be fair to the Oystermouth proprietors, this friction seems to have been occasioned not just by intransigence on their part, but by a succession of high-handed actions by the new contractors including premature requisition of sections of the Oystermouth Railway's land and even the illicit appropriation of sections of the Oystermouth track. However, even more worrying to Morris than these individual instances of commercial arrogance, was a further Parliamentary Act two years later—the Llanelly Railway

THE MUMBLES.

ROBINSONS BRISTOL

10   Single- and double-decked horse-drawn coaches on the Oystermouth Railway, early 1870.

(Extension to Mumbles) Act of 5 July 1865—by which the Llanelly Railway and Dock Company was authorised to extend their line past Blackpill all the way to Oystermouth. Consequently Morris was faced with the prospect of competition along the whole of his line from a new railroad operated by a much more efficient method of mechanical traction.

So why did Morris not respond by attempting to introduce steam traction himself? Having struggled so long to reopen the Oystermouth line, why did he not seek to exploit fully the commercial potential of the railway by introducing *steam* locomotion which was soon to dominate the rest of Britain's railways? Certainly the problem of funding such a change seems to have played its part, perhaps occasioned by the drain on Morris' resources following the reopening of the line. It is likely that having invested so heavily in the restoration of the line to carry horse-drawn trains, he was not in a strong position to compete with a rival company whose sole objective was the introduction of steam traction. Perhaps mindful of the inequality of the approaching battle, Morris attempted to *sell* the Oystermouth Railway in 1864 to

11 Double-decked horse-drawn coach at original Oystermouth terminus, 1870s.

another railway contractor, John Dickson, who wished to make it an extension of the Neath and Brecon Railway he then ran.[6] Dickson struggled for eight months to raise the necessary capital to purchase the railway but eventually failed. It is necessary to record this attempt, however, as the consequences of this abortive deal with John Dickson were to dog the Oystermouth Railway for the next thirty years of its life.

Whatever the reason it became clear that Morris himself was not in a position to introduce steam traction on the Oystermouth line. But with the collapse of his sale to Dickson he seems to have decided on a policy of aggressive retaliation in advance of the competition from

the new line, and actually *increased* the number of horse-drawn trains. From 1869 he ran ten trains in each direction with an additional train on Saturdays and special holidays. He introduced two classes of travel, with first class passengers being transported under cover, and also carried mail on a regular basis; a special Post Coach leaving Swansea at 6 a.m. and again at 12.30 p.m. (the reciprocal service leaving Mumbles at 9 a.m., 2 p.m. and 5 p.m.).

In the event, such precautions were to prove unnecessary, at least as far as the Llanelly Railway and Dock Company were concerned. Their much-feared extension of the Llanelly Railway to the Mumbles never materialised. They suffered financial problems of their own and the pace of construction of their extension had slowed to the point that, in 1873, a subse-

[6] This attempt to realise his assets also suggests that Morris was not in the best of financial health.

20

quent Act of Parliament empowered the Company to *abandon* their scheme. But Morris' celebrations, if he felt so disposed, were to be short-lived. Whether by accident or design, the year 1873 witnessed the appearance of *another* undertaking with a specific interest in the Oystermouth route.

This new venture was headed by George Grant Francis, co-founder with Morris of the Swansea Docks and Mineral Vallies Company in 1855.[7] The new Company was registered on 22 October 1873, under the title of the Swansea Improvements and Tramways Company,[8] with the primary aim of constructing a *street* system of horse-drawn tramways in Swansea. But the Company also wished to integrate the Oystermouth Railway into their system of street tramways and they publicised two objectives with respect to the line; to acquire the Oystermouth Railway by purchase or, failing purchase, to acquire running powers by way of lease. Their ultimate objective vis à vis the Oystermouth line, was the introduction of steam traction.

Steam traction was occupying the minds of many railway operators at this time and for reasons that were not difficult to discern. The Midland Railway, in 1872, had rocked the railway world when it announced its new policy of treating third-class passengers as a source of revenue worthy of encouragement.[9] Hitherto, many steam railways had regarded passengers as little more than a necessary nuisance but the Midland Railway paved the way for an upsurge of interest in passenger traffic and a consequent and rapid expansion of steam-hauled carriages throughout Britain. Such was this interest that Parliament had already felt empowered to pass a new Tramways Act in 1870 expressly limiting the use of

mechanical traction on Britain's tramways. This Act stated that,

> . . . all carriages used on any tramway shall be moved by the power prescribed by the special Act (i.e. that authorising the particular tramway) and where no such power is prescribed, *by animal power only.*[10]

This new Parliamentary Act did not curb the interest in steam traction; the actions of the Midland Railway in 1872 providing a far more accurate pointer to the direction in which railways would develop. But it did make the Oystermouth Railway—whose original Act included a clause allowing the use of mechanical traction—a very attractive property.

Although several engineers were experimenting with steam traction, most particularly Patrick Stirling on the Great Northern Railway and John Grantham on the Wantage Tramway in London, the most important experiments as far as the Oystermouth Railway was concerned, occurred in 1876 when the Falcon Engine Works of Loughborough brought out the 'Henry Hughes tramway type locomotive'. This was given its first public trial on the Leicester Tramways on 27 March 1876. What distinguished this trial from the dozens of others taking place at the time was the character of the man behind it. The engineer, Henry Hughes, was to prove a worthy successor to Richard Trevithick and was to be a pivotal figure in the fight for the wider establishment of steam locomotion. The supporters of the steam cause were to count themselves fortunate in finding not only a brilliant engineer to fight their case but also an astute and shrewd tactician. It was Hughes who first came to grips with the limitations of the Tramways Act of 1870 and who was among the first to realise the importance of finding a tramway that was not subject to this piece of legislation on which his company could establish a regular steam service. It would not have escaped Hughes' notice that the acqui-

[7]Francis had been Mayor of Swansea in 1854, and this leading local businessman was later to become President of the Royal Institution of South Wales.

[8]Hereafter *SI & TC.*

[9]See Harold Pollins, *British Railways: An Industrial History*, David and Charles, Newton Abbott, first published 1904; H. M. Ross, *British Railways, 1904*, for a full description of this event.

[10]Tramways Act of 1870, section 34. (My emphasis).

12 Hughes' Patent Steam Locomotive, 1877. Note the enclosed engine car.

sition of such a line would place his engine at a clear advantage over that of his rivals. It would also not have escaped his notice that a tramway of the type he was looking for was already established at Swansea and Oystermouth.

Meanwhile Francis' SI & TC had proceeded in their attempt to acquire the Oystermouth line. Their attempts to *purchase* the railway had, in fact, failed but they had succeeded in reaching an agreement with George Byng Morris to *lease* the Oystermouth line at a rental of £1,600 per annum. This agreement, dated 9 June 1877, was finalised almost exactly one year after Hughes had first run his experimental steam locomotive in Leicester. Hughes' engineering prowess was later confirmed by subsequent trials in Edinburgh (September 1876), Glasgow (October 1876), Belfast (June 1877) and Dublin (July 1877). His tactical foresight was confirmed when it was revealed that the newly formed SI & TC, who

now controlled the Oystermouth line, were linked closely with the syndicate backing Hughes.

In the light of this fortuitous connection, the precise nature of the agreement between Morris and the SI & TC became of vital importance. This agreement stated that Morris granted the Company 'the full, free and exclusive right to work and use' the Oystermouth Railway 'for twenty-one years'. Morris also granted the Company the right to 'enter upon the tramroad' and all its 'stables, buildings and works connected therewith' and permitted its engineers, contractors and workmen to do such 'repairs, improvements, additions and alterations' as the Company might deem desirable. Should anyone be left in any doubt as to the nature of those 'repairs, improvements, additions and alterations', Francis sent his shareholders a printed circular dated 22 June 1877 informing them of the exclusive contract for the use of the Oyster-mouth Railway and of the alterations it was proposed to make to the railway—alterations that would finally convert the line to steam. Precisely when this information filtered through to a wider audience in Swansea is unclear but it is known that within a very few weeks of the publication of their intentions, the SI & TC had provoked a huge outcry in the town.

In a real sense it was not *just* opposition to steam traction with which the SI & TC had now to contend and it was a little unfortunate that their proposals came to be seen as part of a wider and deeply unpopular trend in the town. At the time of the publication of the Company's plans in 1877, Swansea was already a far cry from the 'gay resort of fashion' describ-ed in 1804. Various factors had forced the pace of this transformation but industrial develop-ment had certainly played its part. At the request of J. H. Vivian, Thomas Telford had designed a new 'cut' from the river, greatly increasing harbour and quay facilities, but thereby encouraging Brunel to run tracks of the Great Western Railway through the town to Swansea's South Dock. The copper works of the Vivians and the giant tinplate operations of the Dillwyns now scarred the banks of the once-picturesque Tawe. Swansea, in conse-quence, had become one of the metallurgical centres of the world as well as a coal-exporting port of considerable significance and though the wealth of the area was fast becoming assured, it was not without its effect on the *character* of Swansea, especially upon the pre-viously elegant quarters around the Mount and the Royal Institution.[11] These areas and further west, around the Dunns and Oyster-mouth village, had become busy commercial thoroughfares packed with carriages, trams and horse-drawn carts bustling about the port's business. It was not surprising that the pace of change forced upon Swansea was unpopular with many of its citizens, and it is not surprising too that steam locomotion came to be seen as yet another threat.

Local protest was soon mobilised. Several prominent citizens including Henry Hussey Vivian (later Lord Swansea), Lewis Llewellyn Dillwyn (Swansea's MP) and the then Mayor of the town, Dr James Rogers, spearheaded a strong and active contingent of hostile opinion. The objections advanced by Dr Rogers characterised the opposition. He com-plained to Francis that the new steam engines were 'dirty, noisy' and would continually run the risk of frightening the town's horses and 'causing danger to life and limb'. Not surpris-ingly these forcefully expressed objections were equally strenuously opposed by the SI & TC. Hughes had already insisted, in evidence to the Select Committee on Tramways (Use of Mechanical Power), that his engine was of a type that could be worked 'without showing any steam, is practically noiseless and shows no smoke as coke is to be used as its fuel'. He had also impressed upon Parliament that his new engine was completely covered in 'similarly to an ordinary car' *(sic)* and conse-quently would not frighten horses any more than any other ordinary car. The locomotive that Hughes was describing was the new tramway locomotive first run in London in 1876 and his claim, that the locomotive showed no steam, arose due to the engine's unique method of condensing the exhaust steam which was patented by Hughes in 1876. This method discharged hot water into a

[11] A contemporary description of Swansea captures, perhaps unwittingly, the features that were the subject of the deepest unpopularity in the town,

'Probably at that time the square mile or so on the banks of the Tawe between Swansea and Morriston was the most wonderful square mile from the indust-rial point of view in the world for there were in it copper, iron, lead, steel, brass, tin plate, silver and other manufactories *(sic)* with collieries, chemical works etc and vast shipping interests. It was a sight never to be forgotten to be escorted over the various huge sheds and smelting furnaces with their carefully guarded secret processes presided over by famous scientific experts. No wonder that Swansea has been spoken of as the ''metallurgical capital of the United Kingdom''.'

William Vincent, *Seen From The Railway Platform: Fifty Years Reminiscences*, London, 1919.

13 Hughes' Patent Steam Locomotive, 1877.

14 The citizens of Swansea resist the approach of steam!

24

15 Hughes' Patent Steam Locomotive in service on the Oystermouth Railway.

receiving tank at a temperature of 170 degrees at which temperature little visible vapour is given off by the discharged water. Its critics in Swansea, however, were not convinced.

The battle raged on in correspondence columns, protest meetings and council chambers throughout the summer of 1877 with neither side apparently impressing the other with the merits of its respective case. The issue seemed deadlocked until Hughes, with a characteristically imaginative intervention, proposed a curious solution. This took the form of a unique experiment to be staged on 16 August 1877. It was proposed that the Hughes' steam locomotive, 'Pioneer', should be attached to two large cars containing over eighty passengers. It would then be run along the railway track at a specified speed of 8 mph. Hughes contended that the protestors would thus have a clear demonstration of the 'monstrosity' they so vehemently opposed

and would be able to determine at first hand its impact on the environment they were so concerned to protect. It is unlikely, however, that even Hughes was prepared for Dr Rogers' own particular test.

Having agreed to take part in Hughes' experiment, Dr Rogers took no part in the proceedings until the steam locomotive had reached its full head of steam at 8 mph. He then brought the head of his horse to within a couple of yards of the moving locomotive, and held the animal steady as the steam locomotive puffed and clattered past. The animal, thus held for fully three or four minutes, never turned a hair. It was to prove the turning point in Hughes' fight. The most decisive test had swung firmly and clearly in his favour and Dr Rogers, for his part, had no alternative but to pronounce himself completely satisfied.

Regular steam traction began on the Oystermouth line the very next day.

Chapter 3

CONFLICTS AND DISPUTES

The establishment of the new steam service on the Oystermouth line was generally believed by its operating Company to herald a new age on the Mumbles Railroad. A completely new system of locomotion had been introduced to the broad agreement of all factions in Swansea. The new steam locomotion would introduce speed and comfort on a line that linked an industrial complex with one of the bourgeoning holiday centres of Wales. There was now only one rail service operating between Swansea and the Mumbles and the novelty of the mode of locomotion could only increase further the attraction of the already renowned scenic ride. As they surveyed the contemporary scene in 1877, Hughes, Francis and the SI & TC must have felt that they had placed the Oystermouth Railway at the very forefront of the new era of development and industry, and they must have felt well placed to reap the advantages of their enterprise.

But sadly—and cruelly for Hughes and Francis —the new circumstances they had fought so hard to bring into being were not to make the new age on the Oystermouth Railway any less turbulent than the last, and ironically it was to be the very attraction of the railway that was to prove their eventual undoing. The SI & TC had certainly succeeded in making the Oystermouth Railway an extremely attractive property; but the consequence of their strenuous efforts on behalf of the Oystermouth line was that the next twenty years saw intense and, at times, bitter competition for the right to operate that line. Perhaps this interest should have been anticipated by Hughes and Francis. What they could not have anticipated was that the origins of this threat to their steam rail service would come from a long forgotten legacy from the railway's past.

It will be remembered that while the rival

Llanelly Railway was under construction in the early 1860s, George Byng Morris, perhaps feeling unable to compete with this new threat to his traffic, had agreed by an indenture of 15 May 1864 to sell his Oystermouth Railway to the railway contractor John Dickson for £25,000. Dickson was at that time in charge of the Neath and Brecon Railway and had planned to integrate the Oystermouth line into a transport network that would link Oystermouth with a series of other lines in and around Swansea. This scheme was to prove abortive due largely to Dickson's inability to raise the purchase price of the Oystermouth line, though Morris certainly did everything to help him in his attempt. When it was clear that Dickson could not raise the necessary capital, Morris even instituted an arrangement whereby Dickson transferred £10,000 of his Neath and Brecon Railway Bonds and £15,000 in shares in another undertaking, the Anglesey Central Railway Company, to Morris as part security for payment for the Oystermouth line. The proposed purchase was thus kept alive while Dickson made further attempts to raise the required capital but even this proved unworkable. A few months later Dickson was adjudicated bankrupt and his shares, correspondingly, became worthless. The Oystermouth Railway remained for the time being in Morris' hands.

Dickson was succeeded in his ambition to acquire the Oystermouth Railway by the SI & TC. This Company had determined to incorporate the Oystermouth Railway into a transport network of street tramways for Swansea and in conjunction with the submission of their Parliamentary application to incorporate their new company, the SI & TC simultaneously published a private prospectus offering an issue of 2,500 shares priced at £10 each, the

16 Extension of line from Oystermouth Mumbles Pier under construction. The photograph is dated 1865. This extension, constructed by John Dickson, was never used.

purpose of which was to *purchase* the Oyster-mouth Railway from its owner, George Byng Morris, for £25,000.

This prospectus still survives as an interesting historical document and provides a detailed and illuminating review of the arrangements then obtaining on the railroad. It gave *traffic* receipts for the period between 1863 and 1873,

	£	s.	d.
1863	3540	19	3
1864	4057	18	8
1865	4240	17	9
1866	n/a		
1867	3818	13	7
1868	3400	5	0
1869	3796	15	4
1870	3601	6	2
1871	3854	1	0
1872	3935	7	7
1873	4896	7	6
Total for 10 years	39142	5	10

The prospectus also stated that each of the line's existing horse-drawn trains took 43 minutes to complete the 5 mile journey from Rutland Street to the Mumbles terminus, that each train comprised one or more carriages with one or two horses to each train, and that each of these carriages was of 'rough and rude construction'! Despite its disadvantages the prospectus not only revealed excellent passenger receipts (see above), but also that the service had been known to carry in excess of *5,000* passengers between Swansea and Mumbles in one day.

Also set out in the prospectus were the SI & TC's plans for 'improvements'. These included the provision of new rolling stock (steam engines) and it was noted that the line's original Act of Incorporation *allowed* for the use of mechanical locomotion. The prospectus also made provision for the consequent introduction of an improved timetable and the provision of goods stations. An innovation on the Oystermouth line—waiting rooms—also figured in the plans as did the adoption of a much more flexible policy of passenger entry points

rather than the rigid six station stops that obtained on the route. The cost of these proposals was estimated at £6,500.

It was clear that the SI & TC saw the Oystermouth line as both under-utilised and under-exploited in its scale of passenger traffic and its virtually abandoned goods service. Their manifesto was thus intended to redress the imbalance between the line's potential and its present achievement. It is likely that Morris himself would have been aware of the shortcomings on his line, but it is unlikely that he was able to raise the capital to implement the improvements required. Ironically, the SI & TC was to experience precisely the same problem.

The total cost of the SI & TC's purchase and improvement policy was given as £31,500, £25,000 of which was to be raised by share subscription and a further £6,500 from private resources. It was to prove a hopeful target. Despite their exhaustive prospectus and impressively detailed policy of improvement, the necessary local money could not be raised to finance this purchase and the SI & TC was forced to abandon its plans for the complete purchase of the Oystermouth line. But it still had plans for the *lease* of the line in hand.

While the Company's prospectus was being canvassed in Swansea the Bill incorporating that Company as a statutory undertaking had been submitted to Parliament. The SI & TC's care in preparing their share prospectus was reflected in this application as, in anticipation of their failure to purchase the Oystermouth line, the Company had already included three important sections into their Act of Incorporation for approval by Parliament. These appeared as sections 95, 96 and 97 of their original Act,

The tramways company and all persons lawfully using its tramways might use the railways or tramroads referred to as the Oystermouth Railway for traffic of all kinds on terms to be agreed or failing agreement fixed by arbitration;

The tramways company might agree with

the owners for the time being of the Oyster-mouth Railway for the purchase or lease of that railway and of the property belonging thereto or connected therewith and of all powers rights privileges and authorities relating to the same;

After the transfer or lease of the Oyster-mouth Railway to the tramways company all rights and authorities conferred by any Act on the transferors or lessors should during the period comprised in the transfer or lease belong to and be vested in the tram-ways company and be lawfully used exercised and enjoyed by it; and

The Oystermouth Railway should for all purposes of tolls rates and charges and all other purposes be part of the tramway undertaking of the tramways company authorised by the Act of 1874.

This Act was duly approved by Parliament on 16 July 1874—at a time it must have become increasingly obvious to the SI & TC that they would not be able to raise the necessary finance to realise their plans. Their foresight in preparing the contingency plans embodied in the above Act therefore appears doubly perspicacious, since the provisions of sections 95, 96 and 97 sanctioned other alternatives whereby the Company would be authorised to *lease* the line from its owners. By an agree-ment of 1 July 1877, the SI & TC duly began to work Morris' Oystermouth line at a rental of £1,600 per annum, and their secondary object-ive of steam traction was introduced by the Company on 17 August that year.

At this point John Dickson appeared on the scene. Though it was now fully twelve years after the date of his original agreement with George Byng Morris, Dickson's return was ostensibly connected with that abortive deal. It is impossible to determine now whether the *real* attraction for Dickson was the opportuni-ties provided by the emergence of steam trac-tion but his renewal of interest in the line at precisely the time the SI & TC were preparing to take charge certainly prompts such specu-lation. His interest, however, was initially

claimed to be less to do with any *future* intentions on his part than a desire to tie up loose ends from his *past*. Just one month after agreement had been reached between Morris and the SI & TC (and the new company's plans had become well-known), a writ was issued on 19 July 1877 on behalf of John Dick-son against Morris and the SI & TC. Dickson was at the time an undeclared bankrupt and one John Stanley Blease had been appointed trustee in bankruptcy for Dickson under the Bankruptcy Act of 1869. This writ made two important claims; that under the terms of the original agreement made between Dickson and Morris in 1865, Dickson had the right to claim completion of his original deal and that, given this right, the attempt of the SI & TC to alter the permanent way of the railway must consequently be halted pending settlement of his claim. Dickson failed in his second writ due largely to Hughes' speed in arranging his steam traction trial on 16 August 1877, less than four weeks after the filing of Dickson's original complaint. The courts, however, had time to consider Dickson's first claim more fully and under the terms of his original agree-ment with Morris, Dickson apparently did have the right to complete his purchase deal. In order that Dickson's affairs could be wound up, the court on 12 October 1877 ruled that the Oystermouth Railway should be put up for auction. Morris, it seems, had agreed to more than he had intended when he committed himself to a purchase deal with John Dickson in 1865!

On 19 October 1877 *The Cambrian* announced that the sale of the Swansea and Oystermouth Railway with all its rights and effects would take place on 31 October under the offices of Edwin Fox and Bousfield in London. The vendor was named as John Stanley Blease of Liverpool and the trustee in this liquidation was named as John Dickson. Charles E. Lee has found this account of the ensuing auction in *The Engineer* of 2 Nov-ember 1877,

Edwin Fox and Bousfield on Wednesday

17 Steam train passing at the *landward* side of the houses between Blackpill and Oystermouth. The extension of 1898 placed the track to the *seaward* side of the houses between these two points.

sold the railway between Swansea and the private seaside resort of its inhabitants, Oystermouth and the Mumbles—places which are known to visitors to the coast of South Wales as not being without attraction, even to others than residents. The railway, or tramroad, is 6 miles in length and there is power to work the same by steam, a very neat locomotive being in use, although horses are more generally used at this season of the year. The auctioneer described the property to be freehold, the permanent way to be in good order, and said that at present the line was worked by a company at a rental of £1,600 a year, but a buyer could probably have actual possession, and work it himself. The first offer was £10,000, and the biddings advanced but slowly up to £20,000 when a somewhat more brisk competition set in, and the property was ultimately sold for £31,000.

It will be noted that this report did not disclose the identity of the persons effecting the pur-

chase. Immediately after the auction these persons formed themselves into a new undertaking later entitled the Swansea and Mumbles Railway Company. Its precise identity became a little clearer when it was revealed that the main shareholders were close friends of John Dickson. The true position became clearer still when the new company put Dickson in charge of their new asset. By a somewhat circuitous, though well-planned route, Dickson was now in sole charge of the Oystermouth line.

But the position was now complicated by the Swansea Improvements and Tramways Act of 1874 and by the lease Morris had granted to that Company in 1877. Dickson's assumption of control in 1878 could not affect the Company's statutory running powers embodied in their Act of 1874 and this meant that there were now *two* separate undertakings licensed to work the same route at the *same* time. Not surprisingly Dickson immediately began to exploit every opportunity to repudiate the SI & TC's tenancy of what was now *his* line.

His first opportunity arose as a result of arrangements instituted by the SI & TC themselves. In connection with their objective of operating an integrated transport system of street and rail services the SI & TC had opened a street tramway system from Gower Street in Swansea to a junction with the Oystermouth Railway near to Blackpill.[1] Consequently it had ceased working the rail section between Rutland Street and Blackpill. This made good sense in the light of the SI & TC's plans for the transport system in Swansea, but it was to prove precisely the opportunity that Dickson needed.

In March 1878 Dickson inaugurated a steam-operated service that began at the original Swansea terminus at Rutland Street—the terminus abandoned by the SI & TC—and ran all the way to Oystermouth. He then followed his exploitation of a gap in the SI & TC's service by capitalising upon a loophole in

[1] This is the point that was later called 'The Slip'.

18   Horse trams and steam trains converge at the Slip.

the original agreement between the Company and Morris. He contended that, under the terms of the agreement, the SI & TC could operate a passenger service but they had no consequent right to operate a *steam* service on the Oystermouth line. The courts accepted this argument and on 17 July 1878, by an order of the Chancery Division of the High Court, the SI & TC were compelled to discontinue their steam service. As a result of Dickson's two-pronged attack the summer of 1878 witnessed *one* company operating *one* steam service on the Oystermouth Railway.

Nevertheless, the SI & TC still had certain statutory rights guaranteed by the Parliamentary Act of 1874 and they had no intention of abandoning those statutory running powers. Though they were forced to accept the High Court's decision to withdraw their steam service they continued to run a horse-drawn

service on the line until October 1878. But having placed them at a considerable disadvantage in the operation of their service, Dickson then attempted throughout the summer of 1878 to force them completely off the line. Dickson served two notices on the SI & TC on 27 August 1878 and on 11 October 1878 to the effect that they now had no right to run *any* carriages on the Oystermouth Railway. In addition, he introduced a new timetable on 1 September 1878 to disrupt further the SI & TC's service. With the validity of their running powers the subject of dispute and their service now in considerable disarray, the SI & TC seems to have complied reluctantly with Dickson's second notice of 11 October and withdrew their carriages from the Oystermouth line.

Had Dickson then *won* his battle? He certainly seemed to think so. In celebration of his victory he introduced four new engines to replace the Hughes tramway engines operated by the SI & TC, the historic machines that had initiated steam traction on the line in August 1877. The new engines comprised four 0—4—0 saddle tank engines with enclosed motion, though whether they were actually welcomed by Dickson's staff is doubtful. They were supplied *without* cabs and had only a weatherboard bent over to form a half-roof, clearly providing no protection when the train was running in reverse on the return journey from Oystermouth to Swansea. But that Dickson should have invested in these new engines a matter of months after assuming control of the line indicates how assured he was of his position in sole control of the Oystermouth Railway.

But the SI & TC were not to give up so easily. Though they had complied with the second notice that Dickson served on them on 11 October 1878, they vigorously pursued legal proceedings to enforce their running powers. They sought protection from the courts for those powers and *won* their suit in the lower court. Dickson appealed to a higher authority against this decision but a judgement of the Railway Commissioners on 9 August 1879 upheld the decision of the lower court although they did agree with Dickson that the SI & TC had no right to operate a *steam* service on the line. They were within their rights, however, to resume working the Oystermouth Railway by *animal* power if they so wished. Dickson, again, was not satisfied and pursued his attempt to repudiate the SI & TC's tenancy through the Queen's Bench Division on 2 March 1880 and the Court of Appeal on 26 April 1880. Both bodies again upheld the original decision of the Railway Commissioners as correct while the Railway Commission themselves, presumably in anticipation of the corroboration of their colleagues, had prepared an Award released on 20 April 1880 setting out in detail the precise terms by which the SI & TC could exercise their statutory running powers. They must have hoped that this Award would settle once and for all the dispute that haunted the line. But it did not settle that dispute; due largely to a succession of unfortunate clauses inserted into the terms of the Award itself. Its main provisions are worth quoting,

It was stated that the tramways company should be at liberty to run a car by means of horse power immediately after every passenger train of the railway company according to the published timetables, and the railway company was directed to make such arrangements as would enable the cars of the tramways company to run behind its trains. If any time the passenger trains of the railway company should be fewer than twelve daily from each end of the railway, the tramway company was to be at liberty to run cars at such further times as it might think fit so as to bring its own journeys up to twelve each way.

All trains run by the railway company which were followed by cars of the tramway company were to take not less than 28 minutes and all tramcars running at times other than the advertised times of the trains were to take not more than 30 minutes in passing between St Helen's Road junction (the Slip) and the terminus at the Mumbles.

If a train running according to the published timetables of the railway company were not followed by a car of the tramway company on at least fourteen days during any month, then during the next succeeding month, and until the expiration of a notice of not less than seven days (such notice to expire on the last day of such next or of some succeeding month) to be given by the tramways company to the railway company of the desire of the tramways company to resume running its cars behind such train, the railway company should not as regards the particular train be required to take 28 minutes in running between St Helen's Road junction and the terminus at the Mumbles.

The maximum length to be occupied at the passing places on the railway by the cars

19 Dickson's steam train, 1881. This replaced the Hughes' Patent Steam Locomotive which introduced steam traction to the Oystermouth Railway in 1877. Note the weatherboard on the cab bent over to provide an ineffective half-roof.

20 Steam train on the Oystermouth Railway, 1880s.

and horses of the tramways company was directed to be 96 ft., and the Commissioners further directed that the cars of the tramways company following a train of the railway company should enter passing places within 2 minutes of the time when, according to the time published by the railway company for such train, the train ought to be at the passing place. If on ten different occasions in the same month any train should be delayed at any passing place more than 2 minutes by reason of the cars of the tramways company not keeping close enough behind the train to enable it to enter the passing place within the 2 minutes, the railway company was to be at liberty to run that train during the next ensuing month between St Helen's Road junction and the Mumbles terminus free from restriction as to speed.

The railway company was ordered and directed to keep the surface between the rails in such a condition as would form a roadway suitable for horses used by the tramways company.

The tramways company was to pay to the railway company for passing over and using the railway, and the works and conveniences belonging to or connected therewith, 2s 9d for every 100 passengers carried by the tramways company over the railway. The tramways company was to render a daily account of the number of passengers carried by it over the railway, and the accounts between the two companies were to be adjusted quarterly. If in any one year the sum to be paid by the tramways company to the railway company for using the railway should not amount to £180, then the tramways company should make up the sum to that total.

If the railway company should fail to perform any of the terms and conditions, or fail to make the required arrangements, the railway company was to forfeit and pay to the tramways company £50 for each instance of failure, and also £20 for every day during which the failure continued.

Though it probably satisfied the SI & TC, careful reading makes clear that this was an astonishing award. Most particularly, the known friction between the two companies seems to have been completely ignored by the Commissioners, especially in the arrangements whereby the horse-drawn cars of the SI & TC would follow immediately *behind* the steam trains of its competitor, which succeeded only in sanctioning the astonishing and potentially highly dangerous spectacle of steam trains and horse carriages racing each other down from Swansea to Southend in order to pick up each other's passengers!

Though it was hardly a fair race as far as the SI & TC were concerned, it was John Dickson who still found the terms of the award totally unacceptable. It was true that under its terms the horse-drawn trains of the SI & TC had to follow the steam carriages of his company, thereby placing the Swansea and Mumbles Railway Company at a clear advantage over its competitor. But to Dickson the *fact* of the award was objectionable in itself; by enshrining the rights of the SI & TC in an official ruling. It will also be noted that a clause in the award foiled at least one of the dubious ploys that Dickson had initiated. Since he operated steam vehicles on the railroad, Dickson obviously had no reason or desire to maintain the track in a condition suitable for horse-drawn vehicles, and it had not escaped Dickson's notice that a judicious neglect of the surface of the track could result in severe damage to the SI & TC's service while leaving his own unaffected. However, according to the provision inserted into the Award of the Railway Commissioners, the Swansea and Mumbles Railway Company was,

... ordered and directed to keep the surface between the rails in such a condition as would form a roadway suitable for horses used by the tramways company.

Thus at least one of Dickson's ploys was frustrated.

What no doubt aggravated the situation for

21 Extension of the line from Oystermouth to Mumbles Pier under construction, 1895.

Dickson—and for the SI & TC—was the increasing popularity of the line at the time their battles were reaching a climax. Traffic receipts were booming and between them the rival companies were carrying in excess of 10,000 passengers per year. This success prompted expansion plans in the minds of both operators and the Award of the Railway Commissioners came to be seen as an obstacle to both. Tension between them was heightened when criticism of their curious working practices began to be aired in the local press,

It was to be regretted that the evening home trains did not run more frequently . . . Of course, the Swansea and Mumbles Company's *(sic)* fine train of 21 carriages and two engines was able to carry a great number of persons at once, but it was too long to leave the remaining crowd standing in the open doorway in the teeth of the east wind waiting for the train from eight o'clock until ten o'clock at night. In this awkward interval as the steam train did not run the horse trams were not allowed to run either and so a great many persons were inconvenienced and their health endangered and many others had to walk home or pay for a seat in one of the breaks plying along the road, although they had taken railway return tickets . . . the older system of running a train every hour is better.[1]

The situation was clearly potentially explosive, and more and more instances of direct confrontation between the steam trains and the horse carriages began to be reported. It was a situation, however, that was not to reach its much-feared climax.

In the latter part of 1884, John Dickson gave up the struggle. Despite every impediment he could place in the way of the SI & TC it must have become increasingly obvious to him that they would continue to operate their horse-drawn carriages on the Oystermouth line, and whether due to a natural disinclination to continue a deadlocked battle or, more likely, to suffer any longer the cash losses occasioned by the distracting competitive presence on the line, he assigned a lease of the line in the autumn of 1884 to two local businessmen, namely Sir John Jones Jenkins, a prominent figure in the Swansea shipping industry, and Robert Capper. Perhaps he hoped they could resolve the situation and run the line more amicably, thereby exploiting fully its potential that had already become apparent under the existing, less than ideal conditions. It is a matter of speculation whether the next step was intended as a disguised olive branch by Dickson or simply an ironic twist in the tale, but these two men now offered to the SI & TC the sub-lease to work the line on their behalf for the duration of their lease. The profits of

[1] *The Cambrian*, 27 July 1860.

22   Work to extend the Mumbles Railway beyond Oystermouth to the Mumbles Pier began in 1892 and in 12 months had reached Southend. This remained the terminus for the next five years. Landaus ran from here to Limeslade. The oyster-dredgers can still be seen on the Mumbles beach at this time.

the sub-lease were to be divided equally between Jenkins and Capper, and the SI & TC. Despite the fact that the SI & TC would now, in effect, be working for the man they had fought in the court and on the railway for 7 years, this arrangement did make commercial sense for both parties. It would be uneconomic for Jenkins and Capper to launch a new service on the Oystermouth line; the SI & TC on the other hand had the expertise and facilities to run the line profitably and had also made it abundantly clear that they were on the line to stay. The SI & TC accepted Jenkins and Capper's arrangements and from 1 July 1885, unhampered and unfettered, again ran steam trains on the Oystermouth Railway. Hence the SI & TC now seemed finally to have achieved their objective of an integrated transport system running a steam service all the way from Rutland Street to Swansea and an additional horse-drawn service through the streets of Swansea to link up with the railway at the Slip. So, had the SI & TC finally won the battle? Unfortunately they had not. Peace reigned for a mere 6½ years.

The primary lease, between Jenkins and Capper and the Swansea and Mumbles Railway Company, was due to expire in 1890. During the greater part of the period prior to the date of expiry it appeared as though the sub-lease between Jenkins and Capper and the SI & TC, which was proving so satisfactory to both parties, would have no difficulty in being renewed. Certainly the period of peace must have come as a welcome change for both operators and passengers alike. But one year before the expiration of the lease, two events of critical importance occurred. First, in 1889, one of the original lessees, Robert Capper, transferred his total interest in the lease to his partner, Sir John Jones Jenkins. This placed Jenkins in the position of sole agent for the railway. In the same year—and it is difficult now to assess whether the two events were deliberately connected—Jenkins acquired a large financial interest in the Swansea and Mumbles Railway Company. On expiration of his lease, Jenkins—now in close association

with Dickson and the Swansea and Mumbles Railway Company—decided to take the running of the line back once more into the hands of that Company, thus cutting the SI & TC out once again from the operation of the steam service on the line. This decision was to herald the most bitter period of conflict the Oystermouth Railway had yet witnessed.

Threatened yet again with being forced off the line, the SI & TC took strong steps to protect and enforce their running powers. The dispute gave rise to a familiar sight as from 1 January 1892, the SI & TC again ran its horse-drawn cars immediately behind the steam trains of Dickson's Swansea and Mumbles Railway Company under the terms and conditions prescribed by the Award of the Railway Commissioners of April 1880. But though the spectacle was familiar, this second period of direct competition differed drastically in character from the first as the friction that had previously only simmered beneath the surface now burst fully into life. Time had not mellowed Dickson's dislike of this compromise and with the reintroduction of the old arrangements he renewed his determined attempts—both legal and illegal—to force the SI & TC off the line.

Details of several of these attempts survive and they became increasingly violent. Though Dickson disclaimed all knowledge of such acts, deep trenches mysteriously appeared between the sleepers of the Oystermouth track making it impossible for the horses of the SI & TC to jog along behind the steam trains of their competitors. 'Repairs' initiated by Dickson's Swansea and Mumbles Railway Company resulted in the spraying of red hot cinders alongside the Oystermouth track again making it impossible for the horse-drawn trams of the SI & TC to operate without running considerable risk of injury to both animals and passengers alike. The wagons containing these cinders, moreover, would often be uncoupled from the steam trains and unloaded in so protracted and leisurely a fashion as to block completely the line once the steam trains had departed. Further, not content with these physical impediments, Dickson also used the actual terms of the Railway Commissioner's Award against the SI & TC, the very Award that was intended to protect them. Under that Award, the SI & TC were obliged to run their cars within two minutes of the Swansea and Mumbles Railway Company's steam trains, but could not operate their horse-drawn cars after any steam train not advertised in the timetable. Dickson, mindful of these conditions, initiated the practice of advertising his statutory twelve trains daily but only for the early morning and late at night with a big gap in between. Its effect was that the SI & TC could not guarantee to have their cars following within two minutes of a non-advertised train running between the 'official' early morning and evening trains. Thus for the busiest period of the day, Dickson succeeded in keeping the SI & TC off the line.

Again the SI & TC were not slow to protest. On 16 September 1892 they applied to the Court of the Railway and Canal Commission claiming that 'acts of the Swansea and Mumbles Railway Company' and its directors and employees constituted infringements of the order of the Railway Commissioners of 18 April 1880. They applied for an immediate injunction restraining the said Company from committing similar breaches in the future, claiming the penalties provided in that 1880 order and claiming a further lump sum of £400 damages. Pending the outcome of their hearing, the Commission published an interim judgement that the SI & TC's vehicles should be allowed to follow *all* the steam trains of its competitors. The Swansea and Mumbles Railway Company immediately filed its counter claim on 3 January 1893.

However, although a potentially explosive situation had yet again arisen, it was once more not to reach a climax. This time though, the reason was crystal clear; for on 13 June 1892, when the legal tussles between Dickson and the SI & TC were reaching their height, John Dickson died. The loss of the redoubtable Mr Dickson was to have a far-reaching effect

on the affairs of the Swansea and Mumbles Railway Company.

Barely a year after Dickson's death a new company was registered in Swansea on 26 July 1893 entitled the Swansea and Mumbles Railways Limited. This new undertaking was registered under a name as close as was legally permissible to Dickson's Swansea and Mumbles Railway Company by the man who had been closely associated with that Company, Sir John Jones Jenkins. In the light of subsequent events the establishment of this new company can be interpreted as heralding a degree of disillusionment with Dickson's former activities on Jenkins' behalf and also, perhaps, a desire to initiate a less antagonistic relationship with Dickson's rivals, the SI & TC. The new company was registered with a nominal capital of £130,000 and immediately bid for the Swansea and Mumbles Railway Company. With Dickson no longer on the scene, they accomplished this takeover with an ease and speed that would have been inconceivable under its former leader. But achieve it they did; and one year after his death, Dickson's Swansea and Mumbles Railway Company had likewise vanished from the Oystermouth scene for ever.

Having acquired the business of the old company, the new Swansea and Mumbles Railways Limited—the head of which had worked satisfactorily with the SI & TC in the past—immediately entered into negotiations with the SI & TC in an effort to settle all outstanding grievances. The new company had automatically been added to the list of defendants by the Railway and Canal Commission but long before the case came to a final hearing negotiations between the Swansea and Mumbles Railways Limited and the SI & TC had led to an agreement. This was embodied in the form of an order of the Railway Commission dated 31 March 1896. This specified that the SI & TC should refrain from exercising its powers under section 95 of its Act of Incorporation for a period of not less than 21 years, i.e. they would refrain from working the Oystermouth line. They would continue, however, to convey through-passengers to the Oystermouth train on their street tramway system from Gower Street to St. Helen's junction to connect with certain specified trains operated by the Swansea and Mumbles Railways Ltd. In return for this concession the Swansea and Mumbles Railways Ltd. undertook to pay 1½d (0.63p) a head for all such through-passengers with the additional proviso that the figure thus paid by the Swansea and Mumbles Railways Ltd to the SI & TC should not fall below £1000 per annum. An additional sum of £1000, as a one-off payment, was also to be paid by the Swansea and Mumbles Railways Ltd., to cover costs and damages incurred in the action. On the publication of this agreement the SI & TC withdrew its horse-drawn trains from the Oystermouth route, and 31 March 1896 thus became yet another historic day in the life of the Oystermouth Railway—the last day that horse-drawn trains worked its route. So Dickson had gone and the SI & TC had agreed to cease working the line; the two old antagonists had disappeared. But though Dickson had vanished from the scene once and for all, it was not quite the *last* that was to be heard of the SI & TC.

The changes in ownership and the lease of the railway were now in danger of obscuring the equally momentous changes that were taking place on the line itself. The *permanent way* had remained largely the same since the line's inception in 1804 but in 1889 a new company, the Mumbles Railway and Pier Company, had been established by Act of Parliament with powers to construct a new railway from the original terminus at Oystermouth along a new stretch of line to Mumbles Head. [2]

The Company was also authorised to construct a deep water pier at Mumbles Head to which the new stretch of line would connect. Construction appears to have begun on 23 May

1892 and a section from Oystermouth to Southend (roughly half the distance) was opened to passenger traffic on 6 May 1893. However the work suffered a number of setbacks and the Mumbles Railway and Pier Company was obliged to apply for two further Parliamentary Acts, in 1892 and 1897, seeking extensions of time to complete construction. Work was finally completed and the extension opened to passenger traffic on 10 May 1898.

Part of this delay was due to a secondary scheme initiated by the Mumbles Railway and Pier Company in the period between 1892 and 1898. The Company applied for, and was granted, the authority to extend the line past Oystermouth and on to Blackpill. The new track would parallel the original Oystermouth line between these points but the fear that this would provoke a period of rivalry similar to that witnessed in the 1860s (when similar proposals had been approved by Parliament) was dispelled immediately by a schedule to the same Act authorising an agreement whereby the Mumbles Railway and Pier Company took over the working of the *entire* Oystermouth line from the Swansea and Mumbles Railways Ltd. This agreement took effect from 1 July 1898 and upon completion of the extension from Oystermouth to Blackpill, the parallel and original track between these points was abandoned in favour of the new line; a change that appears to have met with the approval of passengers and residents alike. The new line now took a more scenic path closer to the foreshore and passed to the *seaward* side of the houses between Blackpill and Oystermouth.

Thus in 1898 a new extension was opened, operated by a new company which was simultaneously completing construction of an improved section of the original route. So, were the affairs of the Oystermouth Railway settled at last? Not quite. The very last years of the nineteenth century held one more twist in the destiny of the railway, a twist that was again to bring to the surface the SI & TC which had ostensibly disappeared from the scene in 1896.

While the Oystermouth Railway had been

[2] There is evidence to suggest that a temporary extension of the line along this route was made in 1812 and there is definite photographic evidence that John Dickson built a second extension to Mumbles Head in 1865 though this does not seem ever to have been used.

Swansea and Mumbles Railway.

ESTABLISHED 1804.

Directors :

Sir JOHN JONES JENKINS, Knight, M.P., The Grange, Swansea.
WILLIAM WILLIAMS, Esq., Morriston.
J. S. BLEASE, Esq , Buxton.

Secretary : E. A. WATKINS. *Manager :* GEO. H. HEMMEN.

Engineer : W. S. MARSH, M. Inst. C.E.

Auditor : D. R. KNOYLE, A.C.A.

Offices: 2, RUTLAND STREET, SWANSEA.

1804.

1896.

This Railway, which is the oldest in Great Britain, runs for five miles along the shore of Swansea Bay, of which the outside passengers have an almost uninterrupted view. The Line is the only means of communication between Swansea and the Mumbles, and, during the summer, carries large parties of excursionists and others from all parts of England and Wales. On Bank Holidays upwards of 17,000 passengers use the Line to visit the lovely Bays and Coast Scenery round about Oystermouth.

It is expected that a deep water Pier will shortly be erected near the Mumbles Head, to enable passengers by boat from Cardiff, Bristol, &c , to land at any state of the tide.

During the Summer a Band plays in the Company's newly-erected Band Stand in Bracelet Bay.

Trains run at frequent intervals.

Time Tables can be had on application at 2, Rutland Street.

23 Advertisement for the Swansea and Mumbles Railway, dated 1896. Within two years the Swansea Improvements and Tramways Company would be back in charge of the line.

experiencing the upheavals of construction, the SI & TC had been experiencing upheavals of their own. From 1896 the Company had attracted the attention of British Electric Traction,[3] a company which had been vigorously promoting systems of electrified street tramways elsewhere in Britain. In 1898 they made a successful bid for a controlling interest in the SI & TC, thereupon effecting the electrification of the SI & TC's street tramway system on 30 June 1900. In addition, in 1898, BET set about acquiring the business of the SI & TC's old operation, the Oystermouth Railway, presumably with the object of electrification also in mind. Perhaps like the SI & TC earlier in the century, they had realised the advantages of a unified transport system for Swansea and the Mumbles. However, the resources and facilities of the new outfit were still not enough to acquire the Oystermouth Railway by means of purchase from its two owners, the Swansea and Mumbles Railways Limited and the Mumbles Railway and Pier Company, but they were to prove sufficient to negotiate an extraordinary lease. By an agreement dated to run from 1 July 1899, and in return for an initial rental of £10,000 per annum, the SI & TC recommenced to work the Oystermouth line on a lease that was to run for not less than 999 years. This last twist in the leasing tale meant that at last, indeed at long, long, last, the Oystermouth Railway was worked by one company under one method of locomotion on one lease for the entire foreseeable future.

[3]Hereafter abbreviated to BET.

Chapter 4

THE HEYDAY OF STEAM

'Tourists in Swansea at the end of the last century and the beginning of this took away with them a vivid recollection of 'that funny little train'. That is how the 'outsider' regarded the steam train which ran the five miles length of the Mumbles Railway—the oldest passenger line in the world. The 50 years over which the Puffing Billy hauled its loaded coaches up and down the short stretch of line from Swansea to Mumbles are, for many old timers, the romantic period of the railway's chequered life. Perhaps this was because the railway had character. It was slow but who cared; it was frequently overcrowded but that was jolly good company; it was uncomfortable —the third class or workmen's coaches were nicknamed cattle trucks—but it did not pay to be fastidious; passengers sitting outside on the top deck were subjected to clouds of acrid black smoke and flying grit —but that was all accepted as part of the excitement.

Frank Gold, 'The Railway Round the Bay', *Evening Post*, 10/6/59.

'A streak of black running alongside the magnificent five miles of yellow sand, rugged limestone cliffs and wooden hinderland' was Landor's description of 'Puffing Billy' as it was affectionately called . . . It was delightful and exciting to ride on one of the 12 open top double-decker carriages despite the slight inconvenience of acrid smoke and grit that would sometimes lodge in the eye and hair. But no one minded for this was part of the great thrill travelling to Mumbles at a steady speed of eight miles an hour. Such a speed may appear to be snail-like in these modern days but it had two great advantages—It only took 19 minutes

to transport you from Rutland Street to the Pier and if you arrived late at Rutland Street and the train was a 100 yards down the road you could always run and jump on to the crowded footboards that extended the whole length of the carriage.

Rowley Davies, ex-Swansea Pictorial Archivist, *Evening Post*, 6/11/75.

The extension to the original Oystermouth line, begun in 1892 and completed in 1898, made the train ride from Rutland Street to Mumbles Head one of the great tourist attractions of the area, and the construction of the new pier at the terminus of the line assured the prominence of Mumbles as one of the great tourist resorts of Wales. Thousands of holiday-makers used the new Mumbles line to visit the resort's impressive new landmark; there to board steamers and enjoy excursion trips across the Bristol Channel or simply to sample the excitement of an 800ft walk out across the sea. The SI & TC pressed home this attraction with an early and extensive programme of improvements to the pier, including the provision of large refreshment rooms, the erection of a concert pavilion and the construction of band stands to attract more crowds. These improvements quadrupled the original cost of construction; the final amount spent on the pier topped £50,000 in place of the estimated £10,000, but it was clearly felt to be worthwhile. The twin attraction of the extended Mumbles line and the new Mumbles pier were to increase the appeal of the seaside resort more than any other combination of events had done before or since and the image of Mumbles as a tiny watering resort, or a modest and decorous retreat, was firmly swept away. The attraction of the resort's new acquisition only increased further the attraction of the

24 Mumbles steam train pulls into its terminus at the Mumbles Pier.

railway that served it and for its part the *Mumbles Railway Centenary Souvenir of 1904*, whilst ostensibly celebrating the railway, was at pains to lay stress on the (mutually beneficial) attraction of the pier,

The Pier has become without doubt the most popular resort in the locality . . . the attractions provided thereon by the Company comprise all that the pleasure seeker can wish for. Amongst the most attractive features during the season are the vocal and international competitions which bring the cream of the musical talent of South Wales. Splendid bands are engaged, whilst an accomplished troupe of troubadours give concerts twice daily. The sacred concerts held on Sunday afternoons and evenings are well patronised enabling as they do the busy worker to enjoy his rest listening in the open air to sweet music while inhaling the health-giving ozone from the Atlantic ocean.

In true Victorian vein, the Souvenir even drew *moral* lessons from the spectacle,

And who can say that in such innocent enjoyments the spirit of true religion may not be preserved and expanded and that in the suggestions afforded by a day's commune with the beauties of nature the toiler is not thereby fitted more adequately for the labour of the coming week?

25 The Mumbles Pier.

Whatever its more ephemeral advantages, it did indeed seem a happy association of amenity and service that had been established in the Mumbles; an association that seemed set to run well into the twentieth century.

For once these portents were to prove correct. Almost as official confirmation of this, in 1904 the Mumbles Railway carried its most prestigious passengers when King Edward VII and Queen Alexandra came by yacht to Swansea and travelled in a specially decorated coach of the Mumbles line to the new Swansea Docks. Here the King performed the ceremony of cutting the first sod of the new King's Dock, which was finally opened to shipping in November 1909. No doubt as a result of the commercial interest of BET in the railway, the two guests were transported in specially built battery cars, first used experimentally on the line in July 1902. These were 'accumulator cars', so-called because the electrical current required to power the cars was obtained from on-board accumulators. They were extravagant affairs of a double-deck bogie design, built to carry 99 passengers in first and second class accommodation. The upper deck was open, seating 28 first and 29 second class passengers, while a special section inside on the lower deck was reserved for six smokers along with 18 first and 18 second class fares. The coaches were decorated in green and gold with teak panelling and

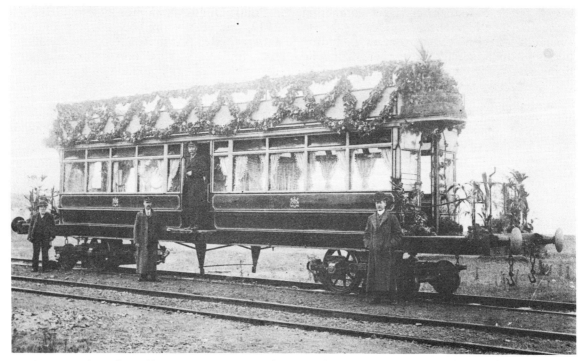

26 Decorated coach used by King Edward VII and Queen Alexandra on a visit to Swansea in July 1904. This coach was an adaptation of the unsuccessful 'accumulator cars' first introduced in 1902.

although they were not commercially successful,[1] they did provide impressive carriages in which to transport the line's first royal guests. One hundred years on from the inauguration of its service the Mumbles Railway, so it seemed, had finally received royal approval. It was a fitting launch to its new age.

In more ways than one this new age was to prove the best-loved and best-remembered period in the history of the Mumbles line. It is significant that many of the staff first employed in the early years of the present century served the railway faithfully throughout the whole of their working lives—indeed, in the case of the four longest-serving members, drivers Frank Dunkin and Alf Williams and conductors Harry Bailey and Owen Davies, only being forced off the line by the closure of the service when all were well past normal retiring age.

Frank Dunkin, for example, began his career on the Oystermouth Railway in the year of that first Royal visit in 1904 when he was fifteen.[2] But his association with the line, as was the case with many of its staff, began much earlier; his first ride on the railway coming at the age of *three*, courtesy of his uncle, George Crook, driver of the Mumbles train in the 1890s. Frank Dunkin was thus able to recall the most bitter period of feuding between the SI & TC and Dickson's Swansea and Mumbles Railway Company with horse-

[1] They were later to have their electrical equipment removed to run as ordinary passenger coaches behind the old steam train.

[2] There was a *second* Royal visit on the Oystermouth line, on 19 July 1920 when King George V and Queen Mary opened the Queen's Dock.

drawn trains and steam carriages competing along the length of the Mumbles track. He even recalled the horses themselves, including his favourite 'Stockings'—and there cannot be many people alive in the 1980s who remember that particular horse from the 1890s! The original Mumbles line actually ran at the landward side of Frank Dunkin's old family home at Number 2, Brooklands, until the 1898 extension placed that section of track between Oystermouth and Blackpill to the seaward side of his home.

Frank Dunkin did not begin in the senior position of driver of the Mumbles train. He began by performing one of the most hazardous and potentially lethal jobs the railway could offer; he would sit perched precariously on the toolbox in front of the engine holding a rope attached to a large bell ready to ring loudly and immediately should there be danger on the line. Two tugs of the bell (later to be replaced by a whistle) and the driver would jam on the brakes of the train.[3] Sadly, however, this early warning system did not prevent frequent casualties amongst animals that did not move off the line quickly enough; the accidents reaching such proportions that the SI & TC were obliged to publish scales of compensation for the animals killed—the most common being donkeys (10s) and cows (£1). It was a compensation that was to be paid quite often in the early 1900s!

[3] Geoffrey Kitchenside has drawn attention to the widespread nature of this phenomenon, and describes well the dangers involved,

> One of the most hair-raising aspects of the early railways was the primitive brakes since there was no such thing as a power brake and there was total reliance on the handbrakes on the locomotive and on selected coaches. Brakesmen seated high upon the coach were positioned at intervals along a train (and) when the driver wanted the brakes applied he would use a whistle signal from the engine for an emergency stop . . . however the brakesmen were rather exposed to cinders from the locomotive and had to avoid hitting their heads on over bridges.

150 Years of Railway Carriages, David and Charles, Newton Abbott, 1981.

Frank Dunkin was promoted to driver in 1912, one year before both Harry Bailey and Owen Davies transferred from their posts on the Mumbles pier to become conductors on the Mumbles train. The close association between the pier and the railway saw several such transfers and there were also corresponding transfers from the street tramway system to the Mumbles Railway. Nevertheless, a 'hard core' of regular staff worked the line in the early years of the present century. Senior guard on the railway in the pre-First World War days was Jack Webborn—described as an 'institution' by all four men who survived with the line until 1960. Then, in descending order of seniority, came Bill Sherlock, Joe Bailey (brother of Harry Bailey), Carl Mock, Roy South and William Zeal, the latter two becoming inspectors in later years. Conductors Sammy Davies and Dai Quirk shared the posts with Harry Bailey and Owen Davies in the years before the First World War. Another conductor who joined that team in 1912 was Will Harries, the previous 'dogsbody' at the Rutland Street terminus who retired in 1958 at the age of 76, only two years before the line closed. Among his jobs at Rutland Street was the ringing of the warning bell five minutes before the Mumbles train was due to depart, sounding notice to the men enjoying their last drinks in the pubs and cafes. Will Harries was also responsible for the refilling of the carbide lamps then attached to the outside of the coaches. These replaced the oil lamps that hung inside the carriages in the nineteenth century, only to be replaced themselves when the line was electrified in 1929. General Manager of the SI & TC, David James, who began with the Oystermouth Railway at the age of 11 in 1880, had his headquarters at Rutland Street along with David Atkins, the general foreman, and Charlie Brice and Sid Thomas, gangers on the Mumbles line. The Oystermouth terminus, however, was more sparsely populated, comprising just stationmaster Bob Millard and porter Jim Martin. Jim Martin, in fact, was an uncle of Bill Martin, an inspector who was working on the line at the

27 Gangers working on the Mumbles line.

time of its closure in 1960 and whose father, Fred Martin, also worked the line at Rutland Street. Part of Jim Martin's duties at Oystermouth at this time included not only the loading and unloading of luggage and merchandise on the Mumbles train, but the distribution (via horse and cart) of fruit, food and even *post* that had come down by train to Swansea! All these men are well remembered today. Perhaps that is because they witnessed a scale of passenger traffic that had never been witnessed before on the Mumbles line and which has rarely been equalled since in the history of rail transport anywhere else in the world.

The scale of traffic was such that on one occasion as many as *twenty* coaches were coupled onto one Mumbles train to transport *1,800* people from Rutland Street to the Mumbles—a record for any passenger service in the world. But such a phenomenal capacity was only made possible by the adaptation and incorporation of several curious, if not unique, features into the design of the Mumbles coaches and trains, and it is these unique features that gave rise to many of the most renowned customs associated with the old steam train.

Perhaps the most celebrated feature of the old train was the 'cattle truck', a large open carriage coupled onto the back of the train into which literally hundreds of people could crowd when the rest of the carriages were full. These contraptions were single-decked, third-class coaches constructed of wood with seats running down each side and down the centre (here being placed back to back). Passengers were also allowed to stand; a practice which gave rise to the name of the carriage. But the best remembered feature of this carriage lay less in its actual design than in its position at

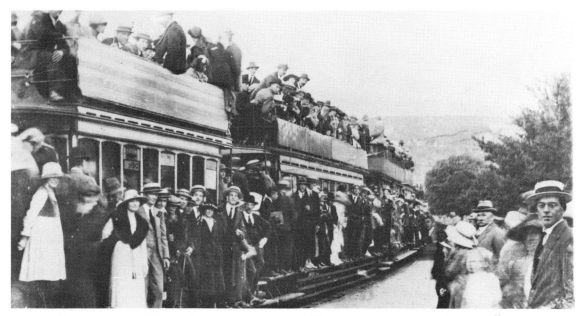

28 'Full-up' on the Mumbles Railway! Passengers would frequently cling to the footboards at the side of the train when the carriages were full.

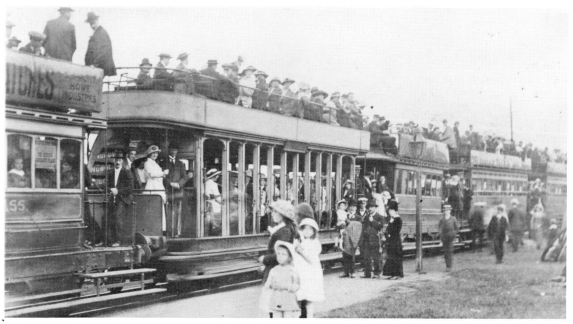

29 These Mumbles cars were built at Britain's 'first tramcar manufactory' at Birkenhead. Similar vehicles were supplied to work as horse-trams in the streets of London, Bristol, Moscow and Tokyo.

30 A Brush-Falcon 0—4—0 tank loco hauls a packed Mumbles train to a stop at Brynmill.

31 Crowds waiting at Oystermouth station on a Sunday for the Mumbles train back to Swansea.

32 School party packed into the Mumbles train 'cattle trucks', 1910. Note the boy sat at the front of the engine to warn the driver of danger on the line.

the back of the train. Not surprisingly the cattle truck suffered from the most extreme degree of air turbulence when the train was in motion. Unsuspecting holidaymakers in the open coach would thus often arrive at the Mumbles pier with their faces almost completely black and their clothes full of cinder ash flung from the engine's exhaust!

The workmen's 'Dummy' on the other hand could be said to suffer equally from the opposite problem. The 'Dummy' was a long, single-deck, covered car with two long seats placed down either side and further seating accommodation placed back to back down the centre. Its most memorable feature was described by Harry Libby, ex-Mayor of Swansea in his book, *The Mixture*,[4]

[4] Harry Libby, *The Mixture: Mumbles and Harry Libby*, 1964.

The 'Dummy' was the workmen's transport of old and one had to possess a weekly ticket to claim the right to travel in it. It had no window that would open and no other ventilation of any kind, and between start and stop it would become literally smoke-filled, the smoke being undoubtedly from old shag tobacco.

It was tolerated however since,

...many authorities of the day (lay authorities of course) justified travelling in that atmosphere by suggesting that that was the way to kill all the germs!

It was not surprising that the coach-laden train set no land speed records on the 5½ mile trip from Rutland Street to Mumbles Pier. Indeed the train's lack of speed—the full journey would take, on occasions, just under an hour—became almost as renowned as its phenomenal passenger-carrying capacity. Local cyclists would hold impromptu races with the train, frequently overtaking it between stops! The Swansea East MP, David Williams, even stated on one occasion that the Mumbles train was actually mentioned in the Bible, 'God made all creeping things', he said, 'and this is one of them'. Both ballads reproduced on pages 55-9 and 152—by Dan Morgan and Ivor Owen Morgan—amusingly highlight this aspect of the service. Nevertheless it was this leisurely pace that gave rise to the most famous of the customs associated with the old steam train.

One such custom that took place at the former Southend terminus was recalled by ex-driver Bill Phillips. Bill Phillips worked on the Mumbles train from 1896 to 1948. 'There was a Board of Trade regulation,' he recalled, 'which made it an offence to show steam, so we had to condense and release it at the end of the trips at Southend and Rutland Street'. Thus a pipe would empty the 400 gallons of boiling water from the steam engine onto the beach at Southend. But on Mondays—wash day—in the Mumbles, a large crowd of women would gather on that beach where the boiling water would be collected in their waiting buckets! On completion of their weekly wash, the clean clothes would then be brought back to dry on the outside of the same pipe. So wash day in the Mumbles was courtesy of the Mumbles train!

But no history of the Mumbles train would be complete without reference to another 'custom' associated with the progress of the train. For as the Mumbles train clanked its way slowly along the Oystermouth track and began its trip down to the pier, gangs of boys would begin to congregate alongside the railway, one between Rutland Street and the Slip,

33 Boys performing tricks by the Mumbles trackside. In peak holiday season a shower of coins thrown by holidaymakers from the train would reward their performance.

34 Boys running alongside the train to perform tricks for the Mumbles holidaymakers.

another between the Slip and Brynmill and so on down to the pier. As the trains packed with holidaymakers approached, the boys would swing into a well-rehearsed and well-loved routine. Cartwheeling and somersaulting, jumping and running, they would start to run alongside the train, performing tricks, acrobatics and gymnastics, and sending up a familiar cry of 'Half-penny o, penny oh!' to the holidaymakers as they clung to the carriages of the train. In peak holiday season a shower of pennies and half-pennies would rain around the boys of the Mumbles trackside, handsomely rewarding their performance. Almost three-quarters of a century later it is the recollection of those performing boys that endures as one of the best-remembered sights from the train's steam era.

The additional attractions increased the number of passengers but this was not without its problems for the staff, particularly for conductors Harry Bailey and Owen Davies. Two conductors would each work one train, sharing the coaches between them and 'working to meet' in the middle. It called for a high degree of manual dexterity, each conductor having to issue up to 41 different kinds of tickets for each stage of the journey with different tickets being issued to first and second class passengers. In addition, the conductors also had to assume the agility of accomplished athletes as they swung along crowded carriages, often resorting to moving along the footboards at the outside of the carriages to collect their fares. Night time was a particularly hazardous time for the conductors since they had to stagger between crowded seats with a lamp in one hand and a bundle of tickets in the other, trying desperately to keep their balance in the ill-lit gloom. And if all that was not hazardous enough, the whole exercise possessed an additional danger on one particular night of the week.

That night was Sunday when the conductors were required to take charge of the 'Drunkeds Express'. Contemporary bye-laws stated that only travellers in Swansea were entitled to drink on a Sunday and they could do so only outside a five-mile limit from the centre of the town. Many local people would thus take the Sunday evening Mumbles train to West Cross and the Currant Tree public house or even beyond that and into Mumbles itself. The Sunday refreshment concluded, that last 10 o'clock train back from Mumbles took on all the characteristics of a holiday excursion, with passengers hanging to the carriages sing-ing and shouting as if in competition with the Mumbles boys! For their part, Mumbles residents became well-acquainted with the sounds of Welsh hymns and Swansea Empire songs disturbing the tranquility of a Sunday evening as the last Mumbles train transported the Swansea revellers home.

The dominant picture that emerges of the Mumbles train in the early 1900s is thus one of peace—if a lively peace—and of prosperity. The promise of the new lease and the new line was clearly holding good for the early years of the twentieth century and as the train steamed into the Edwardian era this stability was to guarantee the most settled period *ever* in the turbulent affairs of the line. Day in and day out, the Mumbles steam train pulled out of Rutland Street and puffed and blowed its way down to Mumbles Pier, weaving itself into the fabric of Swansea life for residents and sight-seers alike. It became a feature and a fixture of

35 Crowds queueing for transport home from the Mumbles. The caption on the card reads 'We Shan't Get Home Till Morning'!

36 Cartoon depicting the popularity of the Mumbles steam train!

37 Mumbles steam locomotive, 1892-1929.

38 Mumbles steam locomotive, 1892-1929.

39 Mumbles steam locomotive, 1892-1929.

54

40 Mumbles steam locomotive, 1892-1929.

local life and a regular source of delight for visitors to the town. It would be out of character, of course, if the history of the Mumbles train had remained so settled for ever; and indeed it did not. But before the train's steam story is finished, Dan Morgan's *Ballad of the Mumbles Railway* provides an affectionate and funny reprise and a fitting farewell to one of the most celebrated eras in the life of the train:

The Station

When we wished to partake of excitement,
That would fill us with joy—more or less
We would save up our cash and prepare for a dash,
On the wonderful Mumbles Express.

The station we start from is striking,
The roof is the sky—overhead.
And flat on the ground—the 'Platform' is found,
The oldest design—so 'tis said.

The booking hall is round in a sidestreet,
A shelter from sunshine—and rain.
And all rushed pell-mell, at the sound of a bell
For then—it was time for our train.

The Train

Our train is a wonder of wonders,
The coaches are gorgeous and grand,
For the dainty design—of the train on this line,
Is easily the best in the land.

The engine—my word! what a beauty
As slowly she snorts from her shed.
Then crosses the road—to take up her load,
And waits for 'The full-steam ahead'.

Some coaches are 'First Class'—some 'Second'
And 'Third Class' and 'Workmen's' as well,
Queer trucks at the rear—all open and bare
And 'no class' at all—I've heard tell.

There are carriages nicknamed 'The Toast Racks',
With leg room for sitters—so slight,
That to sit at one's ease, we've to dove-tail our knees
With the lady or gents opposite.

And that wonderful Van—for the workmen,
If ever we found ourselves there—
With the fumes and the smoke—we would jolly soon choke
And be gurgling and gasping for air.

The Start

The train load is ready and eager for starting,
And steam from the engine is hissing,
The smoke from the funnel causes lots of eye-smarting,
There's hardly a thing that is missing.

The guards—in a row—with their shrill whistles blowing
The engine bell dismally tolling,
When all are impatient to see the train going
More passengers—up we see strolling.

They are then got aboard with shouting and shoving,
And crosswords and swearwords and grunting,
But just as we think to the Mumbles we're moving,
The engine must yet do some shunting.

We hear lots of creaking and bearings a-squeaking,
As backwards and forwards we're bumping;
With pistons a-clanking and whistles a-shrieking,
Soon o'er the first crossing we're jumping.

And this is a picture that's true more or less,
The starting away of the Mumbles Express.

On the Way

We're off at last—the great adventure started.
A tolling bell tells all—we're on the way,
From sleepy Swansea Town we'll soon be parted,
To reach—in time—the Mumbles,
'Cross the bay.

We leave behind the advertising station,
And row of cottages that flank our right,
Then pass the grimy gasworks—with elation!
For soon our pretty (!) prison looms in sight;

And prisoners within are much elated
To hear the great express—and that is all
Whilst we are swiftly passing
So 'tis stated
The 'longest stone' built in the prison wall.

By school and yards and church we're quickly flashing,
And see the waiting people at the 'Slip',
Then by the railway arch you see us dashing,
But 'pull up' for more shunting—on this trip.

They hitch on coaches from Trafalgar Siding,
To lengthen (in short time) this great express.
Impatient are some passengers—there riding,
We'll reach the Mumbles in an hour or less.

At the Slip

At the Slip—what a sight
'Twas a mystery quite
How the thousands of passengers vanished,
From the road—all aboard
On the train they were 'stored'
By a magician's wand they were banished,
No matter the number, the guards ne'er refrain
From finding 'em room—on the old Mumbles Train.

At Brynmill

On once more—to the 'West',
At a speed—near its best,
Brynmill Station our express approaches,
Thousands more—for this train
Which I'm sure must contain
Some invisible extending coaches.
For if hundreds or thousands the guards ne'er complain,
They'll find 'em all room—on the dear Mumbles Train.

Speeding Along

Off—off again on that long (!) stretch of line,
Where each express is proud to show her pace,
From Brynmill Lane to Gipsy's Green is fine,
Here cyclists oft the Mumbles Train would race.

The speed (!) we reached by some was deemed a crime;
Yet bent-back cyclists by us sped,
And reached Blackpill before us many a time
For that's the way our racing men are bred.

An 'L & N' we passed with sweet disdain,
We simply 'left it standing' as they say;
(But here I think it best that I explain
It was a train that ran the other way).

Of course we had to meet the up-town train
At Blackpill Links—where all good golfers play.
Though every 'waiting'—goes against the grain,
We saw two play four holes—'twas worth the stay.

Our trains now pass—the golf house points we reach;
Something's gone wrong—as oftentimes they will.
Folks are much shocked—and passengers—they screech
'We're off the line'—but much too slow to spill.

With levers, spanners, chains and then a jack,
The guards and driver work with eager zest
With bump and jolt we soon regain the track
Then reach Blackpill—to take a little rest.

In the Bay

The half-way reached, we're in the bay,
The most superb in Britain's Isle.
At Lilliput we do not stay,
But dash along the western mile!
The passengers inside—on top,
On stairs and platform look aghast,
And wonder when and where we'll stop
For we are travelling mighty fast.

Our driver knows what he can do
And that the brakes will surely work!
So, for a test—without ado,
He pulls the train up with a jerk;
Folks heads are bumped, some are upset,
Words to express they're at a loss.
No need to flurry—fume—or fret,
The station-master cries 'West Cross'.

On With The Mad Flight

We soon are on the move again,
The rollicking, rumbling Mumbles Train,
And at the speed our engine runs
We pretty soon will reach the Dunns.

That's if our train with such a load
Can keep the rails at Norton Road,
She keeps the track—though speeding fast
And Oystermouth is reached at last.

Here crowds of passengers detrain
Some for their homes—lots for the bays,
To roam the sands beside the main,
Where they oft spend such happy days.

And in the station yard you'll find
Many a horse trap waiting there
Our old friend Peachy—ever kind,
Lifts whip to hat—he seeks a fare.

The engine bell is heard once more,
And on the move—swift! as of yore,
And leave behind dear Oystermouth,
No station like it—north or south.

Upon our right a glimpse is seen
Of tennis courts and bowling green,
Hotels and shops—along the bend
Leads to the sea of Southend.

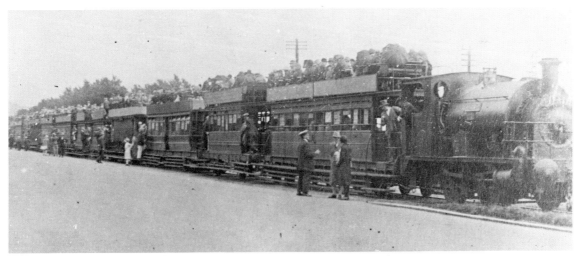

41 Open double-decked tramway-type steam car on the Mumbles Railway, 1907.

42   Steam train approaches Mumbles Head.

43   Steam train arrives.

The End—At Last

Now patient passengers prepare
To leave the train in just a while,
The terminus is very near
We end our journey with a smile.

And those on top—wipe out their eyes
To clear them of dust and grit
That from the engine funnel flies,
(For years we've all endured it).

So we've had our share of excitement
On the wonderful Mumbles Express;
Though we say it with smiles, it has covered six miles
In an hour or so—more or less.

And the pier station, too, is striking,
For the roof is the sky overhead,
But the view all around, is the finest e'er found
In the world—anywhere—so 'tis said.

Chapter 5

THE MUMBLES TRAIN ELECTRIFIED

The early years of the twentieth century may have been a settled and prosperous period for the Mumbles Railway, but it was by no means a static period in the affairs of the line. Throughout this time momentous changes were being planned although they were not, on this occasion, to do with ownership or leasing disputes. They were to do with yet another change of traction for the Mumbles train.

It will be recalled that BET had assumed control of the SI & TC in 1898 and had then obtained a lease of the railway on behalf of that Company from the line's two owners, the Swansea and Mumbles Railways Limited, and the Mumbles Railway and Pier Company. BET was primarily interested in the SI & TC's street tramway system which it proposed to electrify, a policy duly accomplished in 1900. But they were also interested in electrifying the Oystermouth Railway too—though this was not to prove quite so straightforward.

Electrification of the line was not a new idea. Two years before BET took a controlling interest in the SI & TC, the directors of the Swansea and Mumbles Railways Limited had commissioned a report on a proposal to convert the line to electric traction. This had eventually been discounted due principally to the high cost of electricity, quoted by the Swansea Corporation, required to power the track. Upon their assumption of control, BET clearly hoped that they could persuade the Corporation to be more reasonable.

BET's first attempt to electrify the line coincided with the promotion in Swansea of the Gower Light Railway, a new scheme involving the construction of a line from Blackpill to Port Eynon on Gower, powered by electric traction. There was clearly room for co-operation between the two bodies and the Gower Light Railway duly entered into an agreement with BET whereby the latter would work the line, integrating the new service into their street and rail system for a measure of annual rental. This would involve the electrification of at least the street tramway link from Swansea to the Slip, and of the rail section from the Slip to Blackpill; the junction with the proposed new line. BET must have hoped that Corporation approval for this scheme would open the door for the electrification of the rest of the line. Despite vigorous lobbying, however, the Swansea Corporation again proved obdurate. The price quoted for the provision of electric power was, again, uneconomic, and the Gower Light Railway scheme had to be dropped. The Oystermouth Railway, as a consequence, remained steam-worked.

But *why* should the electrification of the Mumbles Railway have been such a priority for BET? Certainly part of the reason was the wish to establish an integrated transport system on both road and rail in the area of Swansea and Mumbles; perhaps to tie up with a larger network of electrified transport systems that BET was busy promoting in the rest of Britain. But it had also become clear that the Oystermouth line *needed* a new system of locomotion and, ironically, it was the very success of the old method of locomotion that was making such a conclusion inescapable.

The old steam locomotives were only partially efficient in transporting the large numbers of passengers that daily wished to use the line. Its somewhat slow progress necessitated the provision of excessively long trains which then ran at infrequent intervals. Any attempt to carry more passengers on the same train led, of course, to even slower journeys. The SI & TC could not even increase the

44 Steam locomotive 'Swansea' on Mumbles Railway.

45 Steam train at halt at the Slip, *circa* 1912.

46 Mumbles train with coaches stretching behind as far as the eye can see.

47 A London-type AEC bus competes with the Mumbles train on the route from Swansea to Oystermouth at the beginning of the 1920s. On the right of the picture is the LNWR main line to the North via Central Wales. On the left of the picture, an electric tram, one of four ex-Leeds cars, waits to return to the town centre.

frequency of service. The line itself was single track for most of its length and had no effective signals of any kind. Thus only one train could run at any one time. In this respect the SI & TC also had to take into account the growing competition posed by the new buses that were running on the nearby Mumbles road, and which in many instances were quicker and more comfortable than the steam trains. Clearly the Oystermouth Railway now needed to provide a service that was faster, more comfortable and also safer than that presently provided. Electric traction seemed to fit the bill.

The SI & TC, backed by BET, having been thwarted by the high cost of electricity, next made an attempt to introduce electric traction by using 'accumulator cars' with the electricity stored onboard in accumulators. But, as noted earlier, these did not prove a success on their experimental run in July 1902, and they were withdrawn from service less than a year later although their gaudy and brightly coloured coaches were retained to run as colourful passenger carriages behind the old steam trains.

After this attempt, the plans for the electrification of the railway dragged on for years, bogged down by apparently insoluble disputes and conflicts over the cost and provision of the vital electric power to the trackside. Eventually the SI & TC managed to stage an important conference in an attempt to resolve the whole issue; to be attended by the Swansea Parliamentary Committee and the Chairman and General Manager of the SI & TC, C. G. Tegetmeier and David James. The SI & TC had sensed a wind of change sweeping through the Swansea Corporation and encouraging

48 Mr. C. G. Tegetmeier, Chairman, Swansea Improvements and Tramways Company.

49 Mr. David James, General Manager, Swansea Improvements and Tramways Company.

remarks by several of its officials had led the SI & TC to hope for more fruitful co-operation than had obtained in the past. The conference seemed perfect in every detail but one. It was fixed for January, 1915; and history now records only too well that other events were taking place in that year to distract attention far away from the affairs of the Oystermouth Railway. The 1914-1918 War, in fact, caused the whole issue to be shelved and the immediate post-war period also did not prove an opportune time for the scheme to be discussed.

One event in 1918 did, however, bode well for the future. At the end of the First World War the local boundaries of Swansea were redrawn and the new Swansea Corporation—the body whose sympathetic stance precipitated the 1915 conference—now took control of the whole area served by the Mumbles Railway. The existence of a local authority whose support of the SI & TC's electrification scheme was already well-known was to prove crucial once the Company decided the time was right to make another attempt to electrify the line.

In 1924 the SI & TC made their move. They made an application in that year to the Ministry of Transport under the Railways (Electrical Power) Order, 1903 and this appli-

50   The Mumbles train served many useful roles during the First World War. In this picture, cans of drinking water are being handed on to the Mumbles train for despatch to a convalescent home for wounded soldiers at Langland. Also clearly visible in the picture is the post box on the outside of the train.

cation seems to have had little difficulty in being approved. The authority to convert the line to electric traction was granted in May 1925 when the Ministry of Transport issued the 'Oystermouth Railway or Tramroad and Mumbles Railway (Electrical Power) Order'. The SI & TC thus now had the required Parliamentary sanction and they also had crucial sympathetic support from the local authorities in Swansea. Their *delay* thus seemed inexplicable at the time. Now, however, it seems clear that the next two years of apparent inactivity was actually spent in dealing with and disposing of the growing *road* competition along the Mumbles route.

It was clearly desirable (from the SI & TC's point of view at least) that a form of co-operation be reached between the rival rail and road services that were beginning to compete for the same trade. In this respect the Company were to count themselves extremely fortunate that a large part of the new motor bus business was being transacted by the motor bus associate of the SI & TC, the South Wales Transport Company.[1] Both outfits were under the financial control of BET. SWTC had ostensibly commenced their service to cater for those districts not adequately served by the Mumbles train and, as a result, BET found themselves in the happy position of virtually controlling both transport routes from Swansea to the Mumbles, though the position was not entirely secure. BET had to make sure that the road service operated by their subsidiary, the SWTC, did not, by virtue of its relative speed and convenience, grow to the point where it would seriously threaten the operation of the railway. The undoubted popularity of the road service can thus be seen to have served a useful warning on the ageing Mumbles train.

In 1927, BET finally began to remedy the situation. In that year they amalgamated the SWTC and the SI & TC under the same roof and the same name—that of the more modern South Wales Transport Company. At a stroke

the road and rail services began to operate from one centre by one management team. It was the first step along a very necessary road.

The SWTC next ran preliminary trials with new electric carriages over the Rutland Street section of the Mumbles line on 6 July 1928. That they were finally able to do this was made possible by the good offices of the Swansea Corporation, who had confirmed their support of the SWTC's electrification scheme by providing electricity for the new line from one of their electricity generating stations. As the current from this generating station was in the form of alternating current at 6,600 volts—the wrong type at far too high a voltage—the Swansea Corporation further sanctioned the construction of a new electricity sub-station at Blackpill to convert the current into the correct direct current at 650 volts, and even lent the SWTC the sum of £24,317 to assist with its construction and other work connected with the supply of power from an overhead cable system.

The SWTC built their new sub-station in 1928 with equipment supplied by the renowned Metropolitan Vickers Electrical Company Limited. This equipment consisted of two 500 kilowatt rotary converters for the transformation of the 6,600 volt alternating current from the Corporation's generating station to feed into the new line. Provision was also made for the later installation of a third rotary converter set—presumably in anticipation of a large increase in passenger traffic. This system was completely automatic being operated initially by the generating station which started automatically the first rotary converter at the sub-station, the second machine cutting in when the load on the line demanded it. Conversely, once that load fell below a certain level, the second rotary converter was automatically disconnected.

With the arrangement for the provision of electricity well in hand, the Company next turned its attention to the provision of new rolling stock. The SWTC approached the Brush Electrical Engineering Company of Loughborough with a list of their require-

[1] Hereafter abbreviated to SWTC.

51   No. 1 Sub-station at Blackpill.

52   Rotary converters in No. 1 Sub-station at Blackpill.

53 Rotary converters in No. 1 Sub-station at Blackpill.

ments and eventually ordered eleven new electric cars to be built to the specification of the new Mumbles line. Each of these cars was planned to carry 106 passengers, 48 on the lower and 58 on the upper deck which made them, in the finest traditions of the Mumbles Railway, the *biggest* electrically driven tramway-type cars ever built for service in the UK. These double-decked covered cars, with a platform and staircase at each end, had one practical feature specially incorporated into the design—both entrances, at the front and back, being placed on the same, landward, side. Comfort was provided by the firm of G. D. Peters and Company who supplied spring upholstered seats in blue antique leather. The electrical equipment that provided the motive power of each coach came by courtesy of the firm of British-Thomson-Houston and con-

54 Mercury arc-rectifier in No. 2 Sub-station at Blackpill.

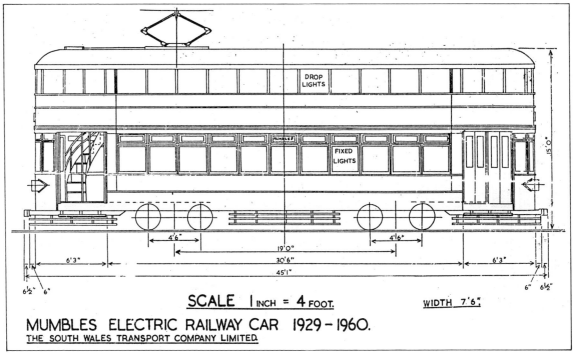

SCALE 1 INCH = 4 FOOT.   WIDTH 7'6".

MUMBLES ELECTRIC RAILWAY CAR 1929-1960.
THE SOUTH WALES TRANSPORT COMPANY LIMITED.

55   Scale plan of new Mumbles electric car.

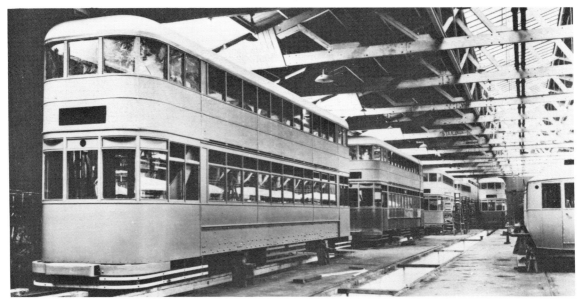

56   Mumbles electric cars under construction at the Brush Electrical Engineering Company Limited, Loughborough, Leicestershire.

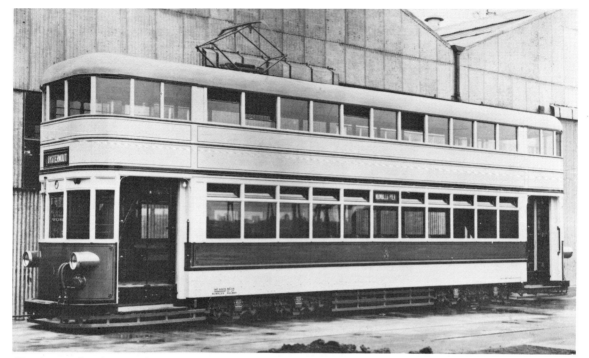

57 A completed Mumbles car at the factory of the Brush Electrical Engineering Company Limited. The original livery as shown was altered in the mid-1930s.

58 Interior of Mumbles electric train.

sisted of two-motor electrical driving equipment, fitted with control mechanism of the electro-magnetically operated contactor type. Braking was also provided by British-Thomson-Houston and came in the form of new air brakes, this system incorporating a dead man's handle, the release of which would not only cut off the supply of power but would also automatically apply the air brakes. Automatic air compressors provided the compressed air for these brakes. Each of the trains weighed some 30 tons and could be driven, as required, on the outward or return journey from either end.

With the provision of electrical power and new rolling stock, electric traction brought with it another new development on the Oystermouth line; the introduction of signalling and safety apparatus. The speed of the electric trains made the haphazard arrangements maintained under steam traction impracticable, and the construction of three new loops along the track, permitting greater frequency of service, made the provision of effective and safe signalling all the more important. An automatic block signal system was thus installed; the signals set by the car's pantograph touching a contact on the overhead trolley wires, thereby energising the signalling circuit. At the same time other light signals were then brought into operation, locking the points at the passing loops and indicating to any drivers on the line of the approach of another train.

By 1929 all the provisions for the introduction of electric traction had been put into effect, and while much of the work was carried out away from Swansea one important feature

59 Interior of Mumbles electric train with driver's cab door open.

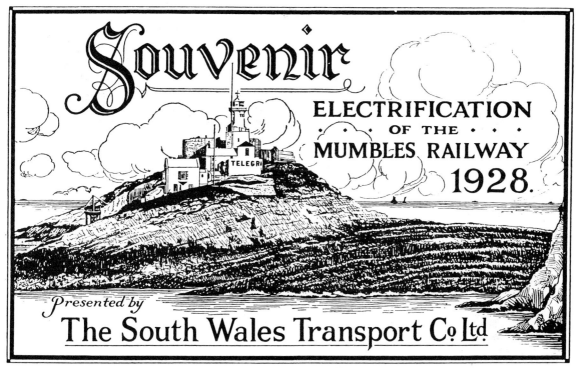

Souvenir

ELECTRIFICATION
· · · OF THE · · ·
MUMBLES RAILWAY
1928.

Presented by
The South Wales Transport Co Ltd

60   Front page of souvenir issued to commemorate the switch to electric traction, 1928.

was provided by the inventiveness of the Chief Engineer of the SWTC, Mr A. Johnston. He devised the method of suspending the overhead wires of the power lines in a way he termed 'diamond staggering', a criss-cross system that overcame many of the difficulties hitherto connected with the efficient provision of electric power in overhead cable systems.

The day of the actual change was fixed for March 1—St David's Day—1929. The last steam train was due to run that day and the new electric trains were to make their appearance the day after. The 'Black Gang' that worked the last steam train were W. Williams, mechanic on the railway for 34 years, H. Davies, driver with 30 years' service, W. Veale, fireman and Owen Davies, conductor, but it was to prove a quiet farewell. At a given time with no ceremony and no parade the last steam train simply disappeared into the Rutland Street shed, ceasing to work the Mumbles line with as little fuss as the last horse-drawn trains had ceased to work in 1896. With as little ceremony and as little parade, the start of a new era began the very next day, as the first electric train came out.

61 Close-up of front of Mumbles electric train. M.U. connections and slot under front for coupler bar are clearly visible.

62 New electric trains in new Rutland Street sheds.

Chapter 6
FACTS, FIGURES AND A TRAIN RIDE

The new electric cars were an instant success on the Oystermouth Railway. The instincts of the SWTC were not to prove mistaken and the Mumbles was soon witnessing another major change in its life as the electric cars completed the process started by their steam-hauled predecessors in opening up the resort still further as a holiday haunt for tourists and day trippers. It began to change the character of Mumbles in another way too. The presence of a unified and integrated transport system operated by clean, efficient and quick electric cars made the resort an increasingly popular *residential* area within easy reach of Swansea; while the SWTC's competitive fare structure, most particularly its special policy of weekly returns, monthly season tickets and special workmen's rates for the early morning trains, prompted increasing numbers of Mumbles men and women to seek employment in Swan-

63   Electric train leaves Rutland Street for the trip to Mumbles Pier.

64   Electric train on journey between Swansea and Mumbles.

65   Mumbles electric train arrives at the Slip.

66 Mumbles train outside new electricity sub-station at Blackpill.

sea town. The service also increased the attraction of the Mumbles pier turning it into a major centre for the social life of the resort. Many of the finest artists of the 1930s appeared at the pier, including Leslie Henson, John Riddings, Carrie Tubb, Edward Arthur and Will Leslie. The pier master, Captain J. Twomey, enhanced the attraction, becoming something of a local legend, his cheery seafaring personality endearing him to tourists and local fishermen alike. The crowds transported to the pier by the train reached evergreater heights during the 1930s to the point where, on one day, 20,000 people visited the pier by land and a further 3,000 arrived by sea; an all-time record! These crowds flocked to the local band concerts and choral competitions, firework displays and acquatic sports

considered by many to be the best in the Bristol Channel. The Mumbles, it was clear, was fast becoming the holiday centre of Wales, a reputation that rested in no small part on the little railway that served it around the bay.

The recorded figures for passenger traffic in this period confirm the success of the line. In 1925 a total of 628,108 passengers had been carried, 140,814 first and 278,528 second class fares, while 14,804 fares had been carried on second class excursion tickets and 247,962 on workmen's tickets. Goods traffic, however, was a mere trickle by this stage with only 8,994 tons of merchandise carried along the Mumbles track.[1] Just over ten years later, in

[1] This consisted of 8,462 tons of coal and just 63 tons of limestone, the remaining 469 tons being 'assorted goods'.

75

67 Mumbles train at speed on the reserved track alongside the Mumbles road. This picture shows clearly the size of these new 106-seater Mumbles cars.

68 The Mumbles train passes underneath the LMS main line to the North via Central Wales which turned inland here, as did a short mineral branch of the Mumbles Railway.

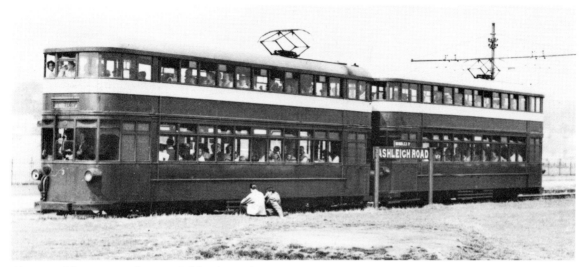
69 Mumbles train at the new Ashleigh Road stop.

70 Mumbles train at Southend under the passenger footbridge outside the Bristol Channel Yacht Club.

71 Mumbles electric train on a journey from Rutland Street.

72 An early morning Mumbles train waits for passengers at the Pier.

1938, the train was carrying 1,192,922 passengers, almost *double* the 1925 figure, of which 972,244 were ordinary one-class fares and 220,678 travelled on special workmen's tickets. Goods traffic, however, had almost entirely ceased, with only 491 tons of merchandise being carried in the full year. Nevertheless, the phenomenal increase in passenger traffic more than compensated for that loss. Moreover, if that figure of a 100% increase seems remarkable, consider the situation obtaining just seven years later, in 1945, when the number of passengers carried on the Mumbles electric railway was to reach 4,995,000!

This vast increase was made possible, in large part, by the speed of the electric trains. The journey from Rutland Street to Mumbles pier was cut to just 19 minutes compared to 35 to 50 minutes during the steam era. The reconstructed track now possessed additional passing places, thereby permitting a greater frequency of service. The new summer timetable made provision for *sixty* weekday journeys each way and *forty* on Sundays. New building work was undertaken; a large depot shed was constructed to hold the electric trains at Rutland Street, the old Norton Road station was reopened and a new stop called Ashleigh Road was placed between Brynmill and Blackpill. This meant that, in all, there were now *ten* stopping places along the line: the Rutland Street terminus; St Helen's (The Slip); Brynmill; Ashleigh Road; Blackpill; West Cross; Norton Road; Oystermouth (The Dunns); Southend; and Mumbles Pier terminus.

So what did all these improvements add up to? What did they all mean? They meant a ride that was literally unforgettable; and leaving aside the facts and figures, the historical record, the battles and disputes; the *real* fascination of the Mumbles Railway lay in the sheer pleasure and excitement of that ride on the train around the bay. While it's a ride that cannot now be experienced, it is a journey that has been recalled and recreated by Wales' most distinguished broadcaster, Wynford Vaughan-Thomas. His special trip on the electric line—the only ride that can now be taken—is reproduced below.

73 Mumbles train coming back through Southend, past the boats drawn up alongside the track. This part of the line ran along the sea shore just above high water mark. The rails in the centre are those from the old steam days, brought into the centre to improve the earth return on single track.

74 Mumbles trains back in Rutland Street terminus. Note the inspection pits and cat walks so that the upper decks of the trains could be washed down.

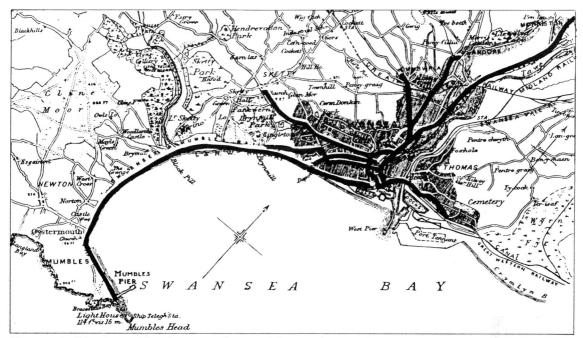

75   Route plan of Mumbles Electric Railway and Swansea Tramways.

76   The Swansea end of the Swansea & Mumbles Railway showing its relationships with other lines in the neighbourhood.

Passenger service is maintained from Rutland Street south-west-ward. For a short distance north-east of Victoria station the ancient line is used by the G.W.R. (as lessee) for goods traffic. The old line along the Strand has been disused for many years.

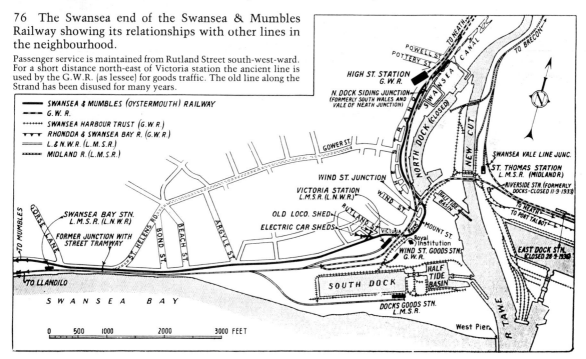

'ROCK'N'ROLL RIDE TO PARADISE'

'The journey began, of course, at Rutland Street and Rutland Street hadn't really changed much since the days of the old steam train even though now the new electric trains were there—the biggest ever built in Europe we were told. They weren't exactly the *fastest* trains in Europe, because the track had also inherited itself from the days of the old steam days and it was definitely a 'Rock'n'roll ride to Paradise' that you got on the Mumbles Railway, even under steam *and* under electric traction! But—clang!—went the doors and away you went, the first stage of the journey taking you from Rutland Street to the Slip.

This was the first *interesting* section of the line; for on your side nearest the sea you had the old LMS train and if you were lucky the trains coincided and you raced along keeping pace with the flyer to Pontarddulais

77

78

throwing steam over its shoulder! But if you turned inland and looked at the town side, there was equally great excitement—you passed the Jail! From the Mumbles train you could just see the upper rows of cells in the Jail and a slightly chastening experience it was. You felt rather sad—must never get there!—whatever you do, must stay out of Jail! But you never *did* stop at the Jail for the Mumbles train took you past, thank God, and took you on to the Slip.

Now the Slip was a more *important* stop than Rutland Street. At Rutland Street you had people from the valleys getting on—even from the Strand!—but there was a better *class* of passenger joined at the Slip, while of course at Brynmill the 'crachach' joined from the Uplands! But the Slip was always a well-patronised stop and even

though the Corporation had built that enormous miniature Forth Road Bridge to carry the holidaymakers over the crowded Mumbles and Gower Road, everybody still patronised the Slip and waited for the gates to be opened on the LMS line to get onto the sands. On Sundays at the Slip, you could also look down from the train and watch the orators on the beach; it was Swansea's Hyde Park Corner was the Slip on Sundays!

From the Slip you went past St. Helen's and there, if you were lucky, you looked up and, if Glamorgan were playing, there would be people on the little railway passenger bridge getting a free peep into Glamorgan. From the train you could never quite see what the score was, the new electric train went a little too fast, so the driver would often just pause for a few seconds to let the

79

cricketing enthusiasts peer into the ground. There was always a large sporting fraternity on the old Mumbles train!

Past St. Helen's you went straight for the Promenade. 'The Prom!';—source of my first amorous adventures in youth! There was a cross-over here where the other trains would be waiting on the nearby line but the Mumbles train went rocking gently along the Promenade. Here the girls walked down one side of the Prom and the boys walked down the other, and muffled voices would come out of the dark,

'Hello!'

'How are you?'

'Going anywhere?'

'There you are'

or

'I don't mind if I do . . .'

and you'd disappear gently along the railwayside and under the Blackpill tunnel . . .

But at Blackpill there was excitement of a quite different kind too. For at wild high tide the great thrill was to watch the sea pouring through the narrower archway under the LMS bridge and then right over the track of the Mumbles Railway; right over the rails of the Mumbles train!

There was no new section of the Prom in those days, of course, so as you looked inland you saw clearly the beauteous delights of Singleton and Singleton Abbey; built, of course, on copper money by the Dillwyns and the Vivians who'd built themselves a very nice little snuggery up there. But at least you could still see the Abbey *as* an Abbey in those days, there wasn't any vast structure of campuses at Swansea University, it was all lovely parkland and rolling green fields. On the *left-hand* side of the track there was now the golf course run by Mr Boon who had a little hut near the bridge which crossed the LMS line into the Clyne valley. There, for sixpence, you could have a round. You had one club only—I think it was called a 'clique' in those days—and you chipped your shots round through the bunkers. One thing was sure; if you could get round Mr Boon's golf course without losing your ball either on the Mumbles railside or the LMS railside, you could really enter yourself for any competition in the world I reckon!

But at Blackpill the LMS line finally left you, crossed over the bridge now pulled down and into the Clyne valley. Then the Mumbles line was alone in its glory; a stop at Blackpill and then off. You were off, in fact, on a rather mysterious section of line as the road had disappeared and in between the road and you were the gardens of houses built in the days when Swansea and the Mumbles was a marina. It was here you first realised the beauty of Swansea Bay with that marvellous curve. The big works hadn't started to grow in those days, the huge Abbey steel works weren't there and none of the great mass of petro-chemical industries had arrived, only the oil works had begun to appear. From those works came one single spiral of smoke and everyone would say 'The oil's down today' as it floated across the Bay.

82

83

84

85

The gardens of houses would then give way to Oystermouth itself. Oystermouth was the original terminus of the line, of course, but with the cutting of the new line right up to the Mumbles pier, the railway went on, the new electric line rocked its way gently past Oystermouth and past Southend. There was a stop at Southend and a bridge over the line, where a certain gentleman weaving gently in the breeze used to join the line in the evenings from the Bristol Channel Yacht Club. A small wave, and the train would pull up, letting the members get gently on, safe and sound from any check by the police on their method of approaching Swansea and Oystermouth!

But then, the final joy and glory, the train rattled on and came to a halt at the pier itself! That pier! Glorious place! The old hall where the 'Palm Court Orchestra' used to play was still there in my day and concerts were still held, dances, of course,

later on. These dances, in fact, would very obligingly stop when the drivers of the train would come in and say 'All aboard, last train going, shut up shop now', and then 'God Save the King' and then the last rush to the train. Then back it would come through the gathering night with people singing on board, back again, happily, down that long roll-call of delicious stops, Oystermouth, Blackpill, Brynmill and the Slip; back safely home to Rutland Street'.

*　　*　　*

86 Bomb-damaged Swansea.

The 1930s, however, were to provide the Mumbles train with another and very *different* role. As recalled by Wynford Vaughan-Thomas, the Mumbles train had already become an established and important amenity in the area of Swansea and Mumbles. But at the close of the decade it was to become a *mainstay* of local life as the Second World War hit Swansea.

The extraordinary passenger figures that were recorded in 1945 were not solely due to the railway's potential as a tourist attraction. The War that began in 1939 devastated much of Swansea in three notorious blitzes during May 1941. Rationing began to force all but essential motor transport off the streets and the raids made the streets increasingly unatt-

ractive to pedestrian traffic. The Mumbles Railway thus began to come into its own. It was not affected by fuel rationing nor, in the main, was it affected by the debris from the raids. Through its vital and crucial link, the Mumbles became a haven for hundreds of bombed-out families and an encampment for much essential military equipment. The Mumbles Railway also catered for the travelling needs of members of the armed forces, schoolchildren and the many hundreds of people who travelled to Mumbles each night from Swansea in an attempt to escape any likely raids from the Luftwaffe. But it provided a still more vital service too. For throughout the blitz, throughout the bombings, throughout the entire duration of the War, the

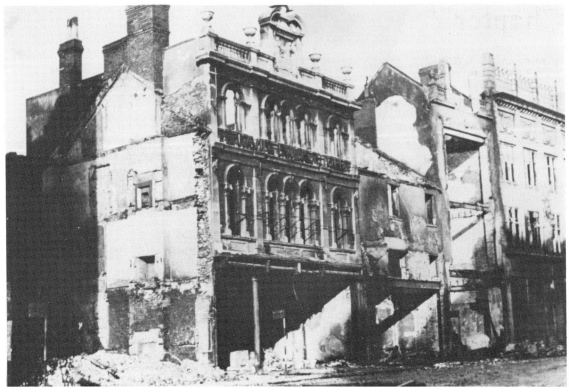

87 Bomb-damaged Swansea.

Mumbles train clattered out of Rutland Street every ten minutes and ran down to Mumbles Pier. Its presence, constant and steady, thus came to assume an importance far beyond even the sterling service it provided. For come what may, Swansea, through its long serving train, seemed to have one transport system that was never going to fail its inhabitants and this bolstered public morale in those difficult War years. The familiar coaches of the Mumbles train became a vital source of comfort and an important and dependable symbol all around the Swansea Bay; and it is probably fair to say that while the service provided by the Mumbles Railway had impressed the citizens of pre-War Swansea, the years of the Second World War secured the train, once and for all, in the hearts of local people.

Chapter 7

150 YEARS OF SERVICE

In 1954 the Swansea and Mumbles Railway was 150 years old. It had run along the Mumbles foreshore for six generations. It had been Swansea's only reliable means of transport through two World Wars and had carried the highest recorded number of passengers anywhere in the world during its steam *and* electric eras. The occasion clearly demanded an impressive celebration. And the SWTC provided just that.

The Company's directors at that time were Messrs W. T. James, OBE (Chairman), R. W. Birch, P. G. Stone-Clark and J. S. Willis, and the General Manager was W. M. Dravers. The Company Secretary was I. M. Smith. Throughout the spring of 1954 these men contacted local schools, charities, business enterprises and theatre groups to request their help in planning and preparing a very special day. It was a day that was to commemorate a line now acknowledged as the oldest passenger-carrying railway in the world and a day that was to celebrate a worldwide phenomenon to which it itself had given birth. The day was fixed for Tuesday, 29 June 1954, a day the SWTC hoped would become renowned throughout Wales. A description of the day's activities illustrates how well the SWTC achieved their aims.

10.15 a.m. on a sunny summer's morning saw the start of an opening series of dance and gymnastic displays by local schools which provided a curtain-raiser to the day's events. Swansea Corporation had declared a school holiday, many local factories also closed for the day and large crowds gathered around the entire length of the railway track. The dance and gymnastic displays welcoming the sightseers had firmly whetted the collective appetite by the time the first major attrac-

Mumbles Railway 150th Anniversary Programme of Events

TUESDAY, 29th JUNE, 1954

THE COMPANY HEREBY GIVES NOTICE THAT ON TUESDAY, 29th JUNE, 1954, THE TRAIN SERVICE BETWEEN RUTLAND STREET AND MUMBLES PIER WILL BE SUSPENDED AFTER THE RUNNING OF THE 9.19 a.m. FROM RUTLAND STREET AND 9.42 a.m. FROM THE PIER, AND WILL BE RESUMED AT 12.55 p.m. FROM RUTLAND STREET AND 1.18 p.m. FROM THE PIER. BETWEEN THESE TIMES A FREQUENT 'BUS SERVICE WILL BE SUBSTITUTED.

10.15–10.40 a.m.	Dancing on the green at Southend by children of the Mumbles Schools.
10.45–11. 0 a.m.	Demonstrations of physical training on the railway line at Southend by boys of Oystermouth Secondary School.
11. 0–11.15 a.m.	Commentary.
11.15 a.m.	Official party will arrive at Southend Station.
11.20–11.50 a.m.	Horse-drawn "train" of the early 19th century will travel from Oystermouth station to Southend. This will be followed by a steam train, to commemorate the transition from horse to steam traction in 1877. To complete the procession, there will be an electric train, representing the introduction of electric traction in 1929.
12. 0 noon	Formal opening of the Mumbles Railway Exhibition at the Pier Hotel by Mr. W. T. James, O.B.E., Chairman of the South Wales Transport Co., Ltd.
12.20–8. 0 p.m.	Mumbles Railway Exhibition at the Pier Hotel open to the public.
12.30– 9. 0 p.m.	The carriages used for the horse and steam trains will be available for inspection at Mumbles Pier.
12.15–12.45 p.m.	Marionette Show at the Casino Ballroom, Newton Road, Mumbles. Admission free.
2.15– 2.45 p.m. 3. 0– 3.30 p.m.	do. do.
3.30– 5. 0 p.m.	Band Concert at Mumbles Pier.
6.30 p.m.	Launching of the lifeboat at Mumbles Pier.
6.30 p.m. onwards	Yacht racing.
7. 0– 8.30 p.m.	Band Concert at Mumbles Pier.
8.0 p.m.–1.0 a.m.	Celebration Dance at Pier Hotel, organised by the Magnet Club. Admission 7/6d.

P.T.O.

88

HISTORICAL DATA

JUNE 29TH, 1804	Incorporated as the Oystermouth Railway and Tramroad Company.
APRIL, 1806	Goods traffic first passed over the line.
MARCH 25TH, 1807	Passenger service started from the Brewery Bank on the Swansea Canal to Castle Hill at Oystermouth, the conveyance being a four-wheeled horse-drawn dandy provided by a contractor. This appears to have been maintained until about 1826, when a turnpike road was constructed between Swansea and Oystermouth.
AUGUST, 1855.	The line, by now virtually derelict, was relaid with edge rails.
JULY 16TH, 1874.	Swansea Improvements and Tramways Company was incorporated by Act of Parliament, with powers to build a system of horse tramways in Swansea and to work over the Oystermouth railway system.
JULY 1ST, 1877.	Swansea Improvements and Tramways Company began to operate the Oystermouth system, in competition with the service already being provided by the owners of the railway.
AUGUST 16TH, 1877.	Steam traction was introduced, though horse-drawn trains also continued to run for many years.
MARCH, 1878.	The Swansea Improvements and Tramways Company opened its street tramway from Gower Street to a junction with the Oystermouth Railway at the Slip.
MARCH 31ST, 1879.	The owners of the Oystermouth Railway turned their business into a limited company, called the Swansea and Mumbles Railway Company Limited.
AUGUST 26TH, 1889.	The Mumbles Railway and Pier Company was incorporated, with powers to build a new railway from the Dunns, Oystermouth, to Mumbles Head, and to construct a pier at the latter place.
MARCH 31ST, 1896.	After nearly 20 years of friction between the Swansea and Mumbles Railway Company and the Swansea Improvements and Tramways Company, about the running of both Companies' trains, an agreement was reached ; as a result the Swansea Improvements and Tramways Company were to refrain from running over the railway, in return for certain payments to be made by the Swansea and Mumbles Railway Company.
MAY 10TH, 1898.	Opening of the Mumbles Pier, and the new line from Oystermouth to Mumbles Head.
JULY 1ST, 1899.	The Railway and Pier Undertakings of the Swansea and Mumbles Railway Company and the Mumbles Railway and Pier Company were leased to the Swansea Improvements and Tramways Company for 999 years.
AUGUST 26TH, 1900.	A new line constructed along the sea shore was opened between Blackpill and Oystermouth, whereupon the old line, which ran alongside the road between the same points, was abandoned.
JANUARY 1ST, 1927.	The Swansea Improvements and Tramways Company transferred its interest in the Mumbles Railway to its associate, the South Wales Transport Company Limited.
MARCH 2ND, 1929.	Electric service introduced on the Swansea and Mumbles Railway.

89 Front page of souvenir brochure issued to commemorate the 150th anniversary of the Mumbles Railway.

tion of the day appeared—an historic procession timed to leave Rutland Street at 11.20 a.m.

This procession was intended by the SWTC to represent all three periods of traction in the life of the Oystermouth Railway. First came a horse-drawn carriage, a reconstruction of the famous Simon Llewellyn coach of the early nineteenth century to represent the introduction of the service in 1807. The drivers and passengers in this coach were dressed in the appropriate period costume, clothed to the very last detail by the painstaking labours of the Costume Department of the Swansea Little Theatre. Next came a wooden model of the old steam engine representing the switch to mechanical traction that occurred in 1877. Once again the driver and passengers were in the appropriate costume of the period. They were followed immediately by one of the new electric cars then in service on the Mumbles line to represent the change to electric traction in 1929. The procession travelled all the way from Rutland Street to Southend, taking half an hour to cover the five mile run, and the spectacle was filmed and recorded by broadcasting organisations all over the world and was seen in countries as far apart as Canada, Australia and Switzerland.[1]

On its arrival at Southend, the Chairman of SWTC, W. T. James, opened a railway exhibition in honour of the line at the Pier Hotel, staying just long enough to perform the opening ceremony before dashing back to the Guildhall in Swansea for the day's formal highlight, the celebration luncheon in the Guildhall.

The guest of honour was Alan Lennox-Boyd, the Minister of Transport and Civil Aviation, and the guest list included almost everybody of note then connected with the railway. The Chairman of BET, H. C. Drayton, was present

[1] Letters had poured into the *Evening Post* after the 1954 celebrations testifying to the celebrations being seen worldwide, in Canada, Australia via newspaper reports and on Buffalo TV news in the USA. The celebrations were even headlined in the *New York Times* (see *Evening Post*, 19/1/60).

90 Historic procession depicting all three major stages in the life of the Mumbles Railway. The front horse-drawn coach is a reconstruction of the Simon Llewellyn coach used in the nineteenth century. The steam train that follows is a model constructed of wood. Bringing up the rear is an electric train then in use on the line. All passengers and officials on the first two trains wore the appropriate period dress.

as were several of its senior staff. Local councillors included T. S. Harris, the Mayor of Swansea, together with many of the Swansea Corporation's staff including the Borough Estate Agent, D. Ivor Saunders. Charles E. Lee who had been the first to document the railway's history was also present at the luncheon. Officials from the British Transport Commission, the Institute of Transport, the

National Union of Railwaymen, the Talyllyn Railway and the Licensing Authority for Public Service Vehicles represented the professional section of the guest list, while representatives from local and national business interests included the Swansea Chamber of Commerce, the Mumbles Chamber of Trade, the Swansea Business Club, the Duke of Beaufort Estates and the Amusement Equipment

91   The old and the new! The first Mumbles train poses by the side of its most recent replacement.

Company (lessees of the Mumbles pier). In addition, the Royal Institution of South Wales was represented as were local publishers, presses, churches and friendly societies. Neither were the members of the railway staff forgotten as Frank Dunkin and Harry Bailey were among the 150-odd guests. To refresh them, the SWTC laid on a luncheon of grapefruit au Maraschino, roast duckling and fresh strawberries and cream, and speeches were delivered by the Minister of Transport, the Chairman of BET, the Chairman of SWTC and the Mayor of Swansea.

The Minister of Transport, in fact, had made a dash by helicopter to attend the luncheon and his desire to witness the day's activities was matched by his strong defence of the unique properties of the line. The Mumbles Railway, he reminded his audience, had been in operation for fully 19 years before the establishment of the much-publicised Stockton and Darlington Railway. He personally had used the train many hundreds of times when he began his political career on Gower, and had seen the service improve to its present 212 seats per train and a train every 8 minutes—a combination of frequency and capacity rarely met with anywhere else in the world. The Chairman of SWTC, W. T. James, confirmed that the Mumbles Railway was indeed the oldest passenger line in the world, and the oldest to retain its independence unaffected by either nationalisation or railway groupings. For his part, the Chairman of BET, H. C.

92   Officials of the South Wales Transport Company sample a more primitive method of passenger traction.

Drayton, spoke warmly of the town of Swansea in terms that made it clear that BET regarded the area as a fitting locale for the home of their most famous historical asset. He had heard nothing but praise of Swansea, he told his audience, as an enterprising and go-ahead town with great industries, a great port and the most progressive of university colleges. But the day's formal declaration was left to the Mayor of Swansea, Alderman T. S. Harris and it was fitting that this great Swansea character should be given the task of summing up the feelings of so many of the citizens of his town. The day they were celebrating, he proclaimed to the guests, was one of the *greatest* in the history of their town. The Mumbles Railway was an example of that progress and enterprise that marches forward and renews its purpose in the face of *any* and *all* opposition!

Outside the Guildhall the celebrations had swung fully into life. Band concerts and dance displays lit up the whole of the western foreshore while yacht races and special lifeboat launches sustained the drama for the crowds that had gathered around the bay. Throughout the afternoon Mumbles villagers in period dress acted as the participants in the procession that had first run that morning, a procession that would transport enthusiasts all day along the Mumbles track. Exhibitions and parades completed a day's programme that was not to end till many hours later when, at the special celebration dance in the Pier Hotel, the crowds, luncheon guests, dignitaries and helpers, were to take part in a dance that was not to end till dawn. It was a fitting monument to the recent spectacular success of the line and a confirmation of the line's enduring appeal that had been Sir John Morris' fervent wish back in 1804. For that one day in 1954 indeed, it was an emotional link with the tiny meeting in Swansea's Bush Inn 150 years before and a vivid and real vindication of the determination of the railway's first chairman to keep the Mumbles line running.

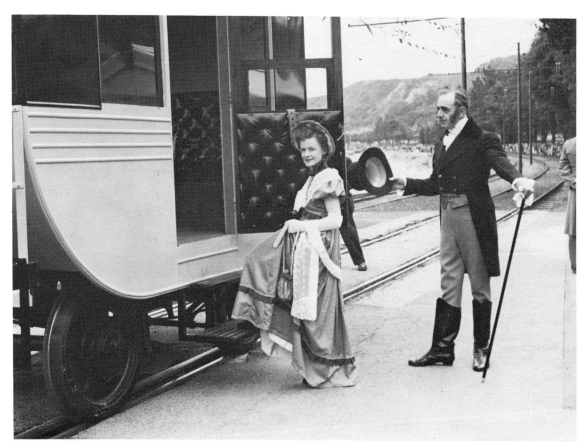

93 A 'nineteenth century lady' is ushered onto the Simon Llewellyn coach. Note the sumptuous interior of the carriage.

94 Driver and passenger pose outside the horse-drawn carriage.

95 Driver, guards and conductor beside the Mumbles steam train. Note the period dress—particularly the Edwardian moustache!—of the driver.

96   Mayor of Swansea, T. S. Harris, meets the driver of the horse-drawn train.

CELEBRATION LUNCHEON

AT THE

GUILDHALL, SWANSEA

IN HONOUR OF THE

150th Anniversary

OF THE

Swansea & Mumbles Railway

29th June, 1954

97   Menu for celebration luncheon in honour of the Mumbles Railway, held in the Guildhall, Swansea.

Mumbles Railway
150th Anniversary Luncheon

GUILDHALL, SWANSEA

29th JUNE, 1954

GUEST LIST

Table		Name		Representing
A.	18	Abberfield	Coun. A.	
C.	9	Bailey	H.	Mumbles Railway staff.
E.	14	Ball	D. G.	Rediffusion, Ltd.
G.	18	Bainbridge	Coun. A.	
E.	9	Berry	Coun. G. E.	
Top	30	Bellingham	R.	Swansea & Mumbles Railway Ltd.
G.	19	Beynon	D. W.	South Wales Transport Co. Ltd.
Top	11	Birch	R. W.	South Wales Transport Co. Ltd.
Top	5	Bowen	T. B., C.B.E., M.A.	Town Clerk, Swansea.
D.	1	Brown	A. E. H.	British Transport Commission.
Top	20	Clark	P. G. Stone	South Wales Transport Co. Ltd.
B.	11	Clarke	David	
G.	7	Concannon	Coun. D. C.	
G.	3	Cope	R. K.	Talyllyn Railway Co.
D.	18	Crews	F. W.	Institute of Transport.
C.	16	Cross	Ald. Mrs. R., J.P.	
G.	1	Davies	Ald. T. R.	
G.	9	Davies	Coun. J. M.	
B.	19	Davies	Coun. L. H.	
B.	1	Davies	T. G., M.B.E.	Western Welsh Omnibus Co. Ltd.
A.	11	Davies	Ald. J. G., O.B.E., J.P.	
B.	12	Davies	W. Tudor	
F.	9	Day	J. Wentworth	
F.	3	Delaney	L. T.	Amusement Equipment Co. Ltd.
D.	16	Dodds	D. G.	South Wales Electricity Board.
Top	8	Dravers	W. M., T.D.	South Wales Transport Co. Ltd.
Top	18	Drayton	H. C.	British Electric Traction Co. Ltd.
D.	11	Dudman	Stanley	Llandudno & Colwyn Bay Electric Railway Co. Ltd.
C.	19	Dunkin	F.	Mumbles Railway staff.
B.	15	Edwards	Coun. A. G.	
Top	25	Ellery	R. J.	British Electric Traction Co. Ltd.
D.	9	Evans	Illtyd Moy	Royal Institution of South Wales.
D.	6	Evans	Ald. D., J.P.	
B.	5	Evans	Coun. T. J.	

98   Section of the guest list for 150th anniversary luncheon.

99   Principal guests at the 150th anniversary luncheon, pictured on the steps of the Guildhall.

100   Mumbles villagers in period dress, entering into the spirit of the festivities.

101   1920s 'flappers' waiting for the procession to arrive!

102   More Mumbles villagers in period dress.

103 Boys performing cartwheels and handstands by the Mumbles steam train, recreating the antics of their forebears some fifty years before.

104 'Washerwoman' waits beside the Mumbles steam train for her bucket to fill with hot water from the engine. At the turn of the century the Mumbles train provided enought hot water for almost the whole of Oystermouth village to do their weekly wash.

105 Mumbles steam train makes its way along the bay. The driver, sat at the front of the engine, is in the same position as the boys would sit at the beginning of the twentieth century, ready to ring the bell to warn the driver of danger on the line.

106 Mrs. Davey, 105 years old, takes a ride in the horse-drawn carriage. Mumbles' oldest inhabitant rides in Mumbles' oldest train!

Chapter 8
THE CLOSURE OF THE LINE

The Mumbles line ran, in fact, for just *six* more years; and in retrospect the 150th anniversary of the Mumbles Railway can be seen to mark the end of another chapter in its story as well as commemorating its beginnings. A bitter and divisive dispute was soon to engulf the affairs of the railway, a dispute that was to issue in the *closure* of the ancient line.

The first hint of this came in a report published in the *Evening Post* of 23 September 1958,

> An offer today by the South Wales Transport Company to buy the 153 year-old

Mumbles Railway is being interpreted in some quarters as the first step in *scrapping* the ancient line. But there was no comment on this from the South Wales Transport Company. Mr H. Weedy, its General Manager, would say nothing of the Company's plans for the future of the line if the offer is accepted.

It is as well to recall the exact position regarding the ownership and lease of the line at this time. Under the terms of the lease, first negotiated in 1899, the SWTC operated the Mumbles line on a 999 year lease from the line's two

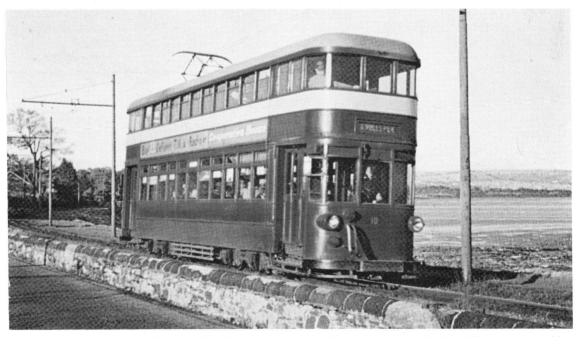

107 A monochrome reproduction of the first in a series of colour postcards of the Mumbles train issued by the Mumbles Railway Company. These are the first colour postcards of the train to appear for more than 25 years.

108   Second in the series of colour prints of the train.

owners, the Swansea and Mumbles Railways Limited and the Mumbles Railway and Pier Company. According to the Stock Exchange Year Book the rental that they paid was £13,900 per annum. So why should the SWTC now wish to alter those arrangements? Their motives were explained by their General Manager in the same article,

> At this stage it is purely and simply a financial transaction. We regard it as a commercial proposition as to whether it pays us to continue paying the rental for another 950 years or to buy it in one lump sum.[1]

Mr. Weedy further dismissed all speculation about any possible plans for the line's closure. 'I think', he said, 'that a lot of people are jumping to conclusions'.[2]

In pursuance of the bid made by the SWTC, the Swansea and Mumbles Railways Limited and the Mumbles Railway and Pier Company considered their offer in September 1958. The terms of that offer were sent to the shareholders by the Chairman of the two proprietary companies, R. K. Bellingham. Its details were,

Swansea and Mumbles Railways Limited,

[1] *Evening Post*, 23 September 1958.

[2] *Evening Post*, 23 September 1958.

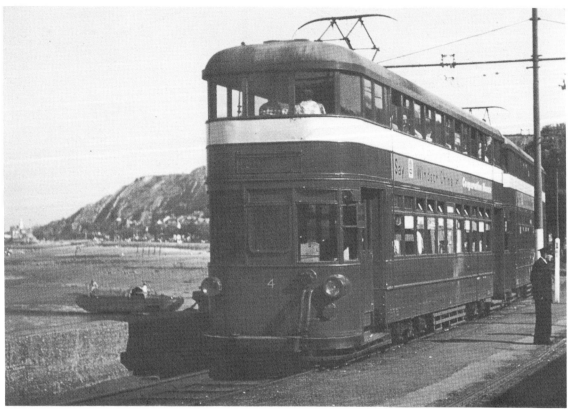

109   Third in the series of colour prints of the train.

For each £10 of the 4 per cent debenture stock, the sum of 18s, for each £10 4½ per cent preference share £8,17/6d, for each £8 ordinary share, £7,17/6d.

Mumbles Railway and Pier Company,
For each £10, 4 per cent preference share,
£7,17/6d,
for each £10 ordinary share (fully paid),
£9,19/6d,
for each £10 ordinary share (£4 paid),
£3,16/0d,
for each £10 ordinary share (£3 paid),
£2,17/0d,
for each £10 ordinary share (£2 paid),
£1,18/0d.

These terms were not ungenerous and the directors of the two parent companies certainly seemed to have been in no doubt as to the worth of the bid. They sent a message to the company's shareholders strongly indicating the course they wished them to follow. This advice was quoted in the *Evening Post* a few days later,

The boards of the companies strongly recommend acceptance of this offer as being in the best interests of the holders of debenture stock and of all classes of shares . . . In giving reasons for their recommended acceptance of this offer, the directors indicate that the amounts named in this offer

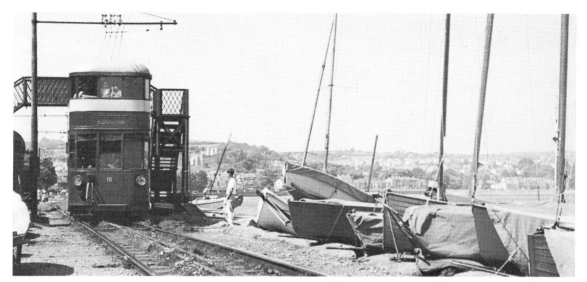

110   Fourth, and most recent colour print of the train issued by the Mumbles Railway Company.

111   'There's a train at the bottom of the garden'. This photograph clearly shows the unique route taken by the Mumbles Railway, on reserved track along the highway by householder's private gardens.

are better than the prices obtained for the shares on sale and transfer during recent years. They suggest that the money recovered by the sale can be reinvested in securities more readily marketable and giving a better return.[3]

In the light of this recommendation the decision of the shareholders was never really in doubt. In October 1958, 90% of the shares of the Swansea and Mumbles Railways Limited and the Mumbles Railway and Pier Company duly passed into the hands of the SWTC. The SWTC were now in sole charge of the Mumbles train.

But why should the SWTC have wanted to achieve that control? Was it, as Mr Weedy alleged, a simple financial issue of the economics of continuing to pay rental against the advantages of purchase? Or did they, as their critics allege, acquire the line simply in order to close it down? Why, after all, should the SWTC *want* to close it down? Who would *benefit* if the SWTC closed the Mumbles line?

[3] *Ibid.*, 25 September 1958.

THE SOUTH WALES TRANSPORT COMPANY, LIMITED
ASSOCIATED WITH THE BRITISH ELECTRIC TRACTION CO. LTD.

Telephone:
Swansea 54956
General Manager
H. Weedy, M.Inst.T.

YOUR REF.
OUR REF.

31, Russell Street,

Swansea.

13th November, 1958.

Dear Sir/Madam,

I enclose two cheque(s) as detailed hereunder in consideration for the transfer to the Company of your undermentioned holdings.

Yours faithfully,
THE SOUTH WALES TRANSPORT COMPANY LIMITED

Secretary,

The Mumbles Railway & Pier Company
Preference Shares   £
Ordinary Shares   9.19.6   £ 9.19.6

The Swansea & Mumbles Railways Limited
Debenture Stock   £
Preference Shares   £ 8.14.6
Ordinary Shares   £ 8.17.6

Miss M.D. Phillips.

112 Actual letter received by Mumbles Railway shareholder in 1958 containing the bid of the South Wales Transport Company for the shares in the Mumbles train.

BET would—the parent company of SWTC—and by 1958 one of the country's largest operators of motor buses.

The debate was not left unresolved for long. A mere month after the SWTC assumed control of the Mumbles Railway, an application on behalf of the Company was submitted to the House of Lords. This application was entitled the South Wales Transport Bill, and the SWTC matched the ambiguity of this title with a discreet silence about its intentions. Consequently undetected and unobserved by any interested party, the SWTC's Bill passed its first reading in the Upper House. There is, indeed, no reason to assume that its second reading would have again been anything but a formality had it not been for the diligence of two peers, Lords Merrivale and Ogmore. These peers, alerted by rumours in Swansea and Mumbles, investigated and divined the real purpose of the application that was proceeding unhampered through the Chamber. Its purpose, they discovered, was to *close* the Mumbles Railway.

Reaction in Swansea and Mumbles was instantaneous. From November 1958 the area witnessed an explosion of protest and a sustained and constant period of agitation against the SWTC's plans to close the line. Various national organisations took an interest, including the Light Railway Transport League[4] who were fighting similar battles to keep lines running in other parts of the UK. Within days a Mumbles Railway Passenger Association was formed under the Chairmanship of John Woods, local representative of the LRTL, and containing among its membership representatives of many influential local bodies, including local Chambers of Trade. This determined and highly motivated band of people immediately began to organise protest meetings along the length of Swansea Bay, publishing pamphlets and leaflets calling for the line to be retained and setting in motion a petition against the proposed closure that would eventually raise 14,000 signatures.

[4] Hereafter abbreviated to LRTL.

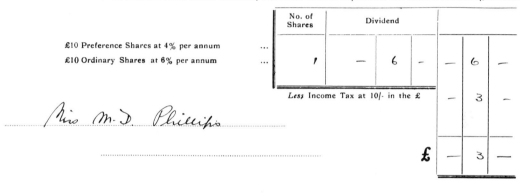

Mumbles Railway and Pier Company.

MUMBLES, FEB. **1943.**

Enclosed I have the pleasure of handing you Cheque for Dividend for the Half year ending Dec. 31st, 1942, as per subjoined particulars.

I hereby certify that the Income Tax as shewn herein has been or will be duly paid to the proper officer for the receipt of Taxes on the property of the Mumbles Railway and Pier Co., and the Swansea and Mumbles Railways, Limited, situate at London.

Any alteration of your address should be immediately notified to the Secretary.

E. A. WATKINS,

Secretary.

N.B.—Proprietors who are entitled to exemption or abatement in respect of Income Tax are requested to retain this Statement, which will be received by the Inland Revenue Department as a voucher on claiming the same

	No. of Shares	Dividend				
£10 Preference Shares at 4% per annum ...						
£10 Ordinary Shares at 6% per annum ...	1	— 6	-	—	6	—
		Less Income Tax at 10/- in the £		—	3	—
Mrs M. D. Phillips						
			£	—	3	—

113   Dividend certificate for the Mumbles Railway and Pier Company, February 1943.

Letters began to pour into the area in support of the fight from countries as far afield as India, Australia, New Zealand and South Africa, all of which were forwarded to the appropriate authorities. Petitions linked to the major petition in Mumbles were organised throughout Wales and in April 1959 the largest public meeting held in the Beaufort Hall in Swansea forwarded a formal resolution to the SWTC and to Lord Brecon, the Secretary of State for Wales, deploring the action of the SWTC in attempting to close the Mumbles line and urging the Company to retain and modernise the service provided by the Mumbles train. All this time the SWTC refused to take part in any of the protest meetings or indeed to debate the issue or take account of the strong local feeling. They rested solely on their previous statement that they believed the transport system for the people of Swansea and the Mumbles would be improved immeasurably by the substitution of motor buses for the Mumbles train.

The protest movement that emerged in Swansea and Mumbles in the latter part of 1958 and which continued through the early

Swansea and Mumbles Railways Ltd.

MUMBLES, FEB. **1943.**

Enclosed I have the pleasure of handing you Cheque for Dividend for the Half year ending Dec. 31st, 1942, as per subjoined particulars.

I hereby certify that the Income Tax as shewn herein has been or will be duly paid to the proper officer for the receipt of Taxes on the property of the Mumbles Railway and Pier Co., and the Swansea and Mumbles Railways, Limited, situate at London.

Any alteration of your address should be immediately notified to the Secretary.

E. A. WATKINS,

Secretary.

N.B.—Proprietors who are entitled to exemption or abatement in respect of Income Tax are requested to retain this Statement, which will be received by the Inland Revenue Department as a voucher on claiming the same

	No. of Shares	Dividend			
£10 Preference Shares at 4½% per annum ...	1	—	4	6	
£8 Ordinary Shares at 7½% per annum ...				4	6
Less Income Tax at 10/- in the £				2	3
Mrs M. D. Phillips			£ —	2	3

114   Dividend certificate for the Swansea and Mumbles Railways Limited, February 1943.

months of 1959, was well-organised, voluble and, as far as it went, effective. But on its own it was never going to be enough and as 1958 passed into 1959 it became obvious to the protestors that they had to fight the SWTC on their *own* terms; they had to fight the SWTC in Parliament and block the passage of the Company's Bill as it attempted to progress through the House of Commons and the House of Lords. That was precisely what they set out to do.

The protest movement first had to acquaint themselves with the Parliamentary process.

This process divides Bills into roughly two sorts; public and private. The former are usually introduced by the Government and are the best publicised Bills of any Parliamentary session. Private Bills, such as the South Wales Transport Bill, are generally those introduced by private companies or by individuals for their own particular purposes and, in general, they receive little or no publicity. Having been introduced, Parliamentary Bills then have to pass both Houses of Parliament, though in what order they are submitted is left to the sponsor of the Bill. In each House they have to

Keep the MUMBLES RAILWAY running!

The Mumbles Railway is unique. It is the world's oldest passenger railway and one of Britain's few electric light railways.

But it is not a museum piece. It is capable of being developed as a modern high-speed line to give fast and safe travel, free from the congestion of the streets.

In other parts of the world such lines play an important part in urban and suburban transport.

A modern Continental articulated light railway car.

CONSIDER THESE FACTS:

A two-car train on the Mumbles Railway can carry some 250 passengers with a crew of three. To replace one of these trains would require four buses and a crew of eight.

The trains run in safety on their own right of way, unimpeded and clear of other traffic.

The Railway uses electricity generated from home-produced fuel, and is not dependent on imported oil.

The Mumbles Railway provides a unique seaside ride along the sweeping curve of Swansea Bay. To visitors it is the favourite way of seeing this fine panorama and of reaching the resorts of Oystermouth and Mumbles. If the railway were closed the Bay would lose one of its attractions.

A substituting bus route would not offer the holiday public the same attraction. A bus is a bus whether it is in Swansea, Sheffield, Southampton or other large towns.

A substituting bus service would require thousands spent on road construction **at the expense of the ratepayers.**

The railway has long been part of the local scene; it still has an important part to play in local transport and in the development of Swansea Bay. Help by using the railway as much as possible; a frequent service of trains is operated. Let it show what it can do!

The Mumbles Railway has a long and distinguished past; it can also have a successful future.

KEEP the Mumbles RAILWAY RUNNING.

Published by the Light Railway Transport League and printed by W. J. Fowler & Son, Ltd., 245, Cricklewood Broadway, N.W.2

115 Illustrated handbill printed in the winter of 1958/9. 'Keep the MUMBLES RAILWAY running!'

undergo a first reading, a second reading, a Committee stage, a report stage and, finally, a third reading. Any amendments made in one House must be agreed to by the other House. Only after a Bill has passed all its stages and all amendments have been agreed by both Houses, can a Bill be given Royal Assent. The Parliamentary process thus seems to discourage all but the most worthy legislation to progress through the two Houses. That, at least, was the hope of the objectors to the South Wales Transport Bill back in Swansea.

The SWTC chose first to submit their Bill to the House of Lords and the lack of publicity accompanied by the discreet silence of its sponsors, ensured that the first reading was a formality. The second reading would have followed a similar pattern had it not been for the diligence of the two peers who then rose to condemn it. As a consequence of the strong feeling expressed, the second reading was postponed for 12 days but was eventually allowed to proceed to its committee stage on the understanding that the protest could there be more effectively assessed. The committee hearing was scheduled for May 1959 and seemed to be the *major* chance for the protest movement to present their case.

There were problems, however, that the protest movement had first to overcome. Most particularly, they had the problem of actually *appearing* before the Parliamentary Committee. The right to give evidence was limited, by the rules that govern such committees, to those individuals and bodies whose property or pecuniary interests may be affected by its passage. Thus, organisations like the LRTL, with their dedicated and well-organised membership, would be *excluded*. It is true that the ordinary Swansea commuter would not have been excluded from the hearing but, as the LRTL pointed out, he would have to read and inwardly digest the 1,139 pages of the current edition of Sir T. Erskine May's *Treatise on the Law, Privileges, Proceedings and Usage of Parliament* to acquaint himself with his rights and then to have employed solicitors, parliamentary agents, parliament-

116 Opponents of the plans to scrap the Mumbles train advertise public meeting, May 1959.

ary counsel and sundry other experts required to assist him to fight his case and represent his protest. Not surprisingly perhaps, no such Swansea commuter appeared.

However, two main bodies did apply for and were granted the right to appear before the committee. The first was the Amusement Equipment Company, the lessees of the Mumbles Hotel and pier from the SWTC. They were alarmed at the potential decline in business that they felt would result from the abandonment of the railway that terminated at that pier. Thus they found themselves in the somewhat invidious position of petitioning against the very body that sanctioned their lease. The second body to petition against the Bill was the Swansea Corporation. The chief witness for the Amusement Equipment

Company was Jack Bartlett, manager of the Mumbles pier and Hotel. Along with other officials from the company, Jack Bartlett had been instrumental in the many public meetings and petitions organised in the area from November 1958 onwards and, in common with many others, he saw his trip to the House of Lords as the culmination of the protest campaign he had helped to foment. It had been a well-prepared and well-organised campaign thus far, but it was to go very, very wrong.

The author conducted a series of interviews with Jack Bartlett in January, 1982. He had long retired from his post with the Amusement Equipment Company but his memory of the events of that time remained crystal clear. His recollections of how their campaign went awry now makes astonishing reading.

Tel. Glastonbury 3239 .

GLASLYN.
35, TOR VIEW AVENUE.
GLASTONBURY. Som.
4th October,1959

CONFIDENTIAL & PRIVILEGED.

Mrs. W. BARRINGTON,
"Beverley"
Queens Rd., MUMBLES. Swansea.

Dear Mrs. Barrington,

Swansea and Mumbles Light Railway.

You will have heard from Mr. Bishop, the Secretary of Swansea Chamber of Commerce who has I hope, by this time, passed on my letter to him, to you.

I have been interested in Electric Light Railways for very many years and I am sorry to have to confess that it was not until 10 days ago that I made the journey to Swansea and travelled on your excellent Swansea and Mumbles Light Railway. What on earth are they closing it for? Surely it is one of the assets of the district? Can nothing be done to preserve it?

In a short visit, I formed the following opinion. (a) The rolling-stock is in sturdy condition and the two damaged cars could easily be repaired (b) no maintenance has purposely been done on the track for a long time and all the fishplates need tightening up, this would improve the side-roll tremendously (c) the line is a scenic one, like Blackpool (which makes a huge profit) and there are no heavy gradients to cause unnecessary strain on the equipment (d) the track has many years wear in it and only needs re-alignment (due entirely to lack of maintenance) (e) the cars also have, at least, another 20/30 years wear in them (longer judging by Glasgow system) (f) the electrical equipment seemed, to me, to be very adequate for the traffic.

If, as I was told, Swansea wants the line for promenade extension, is there any reason why this extension could not incorporate the line in it, as has been done with such excellent results at Blackpool, which is an apposite?

I formed the opinion, from talking to employees of the Light Railway that they are loyal but they seem to have been indoctrinated with "omnibus reasons" for the abandonment of the line. Do Swansea people realise that assurances that the fares will not go up when the line is abandoned are worthless, as is proved by many past cases of similar abandonments.

What do you think would be the local reaction to the formation of a Swansea and Mumbles Light Railway Preservation Society, as has been done with two light railways in North Wales and also you will have read of the £72,000 raised to preserve the Bluebell Line, in Kent? All of these three railways had been abandoned but yours is a going concern and very much alive. Much could be done in the way of effecting economies and I am sure that, as a business-man, a Preservation Society, with a strong policy would be able to do much.

It is quite certain that buses will never be able to cope with the crowds which the Bay so obviously attracts, at holiday times. I know the Light Railway is being cut-back to Oystermouth on the 12th of this month but, even so, there will still be a lot of it left, on a remunerative section of the line.

Did you know that a Preservation Society was formed to try and save the Llandudno Tramway, four years ago and raised £7,000 but were beaten by bad negotiations. This latter tramway WAS IN A VERY BAD CONDITION and would have required a huge sum to set it up but, even so, one of the assets of Llandudno and Colwyn Bay is now finished and the visitors have diminished accordingly .....because, after all, one can ride on a bus anywhere in England and there is not much point in seeing the views from the top of a bus when one can do this anywhere. Also, the population of Llandudno is only 17,000 whilst the polulation of Swansea is 162,000. This leads me to assume that there may be enough local business-men to support the retention of the Light Railway.....co-operating with and meeting Swansea on their Promenade Extension also, to the benefit of both Swansea and the visitors.

For your guidance, the Festiniog Railway Preservation Society and the Tallylyn Railway Preservation Society have raised considerable sums, at Exhibitions at which I have been present, to reconstruct these two Light Railways (they were derelict!) and there is considerably more traffic on the Swansea and Mumbles Light Railway than these two mentioned railways will ever carry! In the case of the Tallylyn, they even got the R.E's (territorials) to do the track work for them, as a summer exercise!

I am sure that there must be a body of men of goodwill in your area who can review the position again. I will, willingly, give them the benefit of my experience which is not inconsiderable, on these matters. Meanwhile, can you let me have some newspaper cuttings and a recent balance sheet of the Company?

Could I ask you to treat this matter as confidential for the time being?

Yours sincerely,

E. Jackson Stevens .

117 Just one of the many hundreds of letters received by the Mumbles Railway Passenger Association, objecting to SWTC's plans to scrap the historic Mumbles line.

According to Jack Bartlett, the directors of the Amusement Equipment Company came from all parts of Britain in order to attend the House of Lords hearing and had arranged to meet in their counsel's chambers at Whitehall at five o'clock the night before to be briefed by their barrister on the tactics and procedure for the following day. This, of course, was standard procedure. Jack Bartlett was to be called as chief witness to testify to the damaging effects of the withdrawal of the Mumbles service. The Amusement Equipment Company had pre-pared their case well and the company's legal counsel was to use Jack Bartlett's evidence to present a cogent and well-documented case against the closure of the Swansea and Mumbles line. But what happened next was to *wreck* those carefully-planned tactics. For those directors and staff, duly assembled in counsel's chambers and waiting for their legal counsel, waited for that counsel in *vain*. After an increasingly nervous interval a note was handed to the Chairman of the Amusement Equipment Company informing him that

118 Mumbles train approaches along that 'long and splendid shore' as Dylan Thomas described it.

120 Mumbles train by the bay.

119 Another example of the scenic route taken by the Mumbles train.

121   Mumbles train by the Swansea University complex.

their counsel had simply and very abruptly *quit* their case.

The implications of Jack Bartlett's astonishing testimony should be made absolutely clear. According to the chief witness for the Amusement Equipment Company, the Company was left without *any* legal representation a matter of hours before their evidence was due to be heard. The Company had then to search frantically for a replacement counsel, engage him at short notice and brief him hurriedly for a case that was due to start the following morning. That the Company actually achieved this is remarkable. If he had been as effective as they hoped the original counsel would

prove, that would have been even more remarkable. But in the circumstances that would have been too much to ask.

The committee hearing was held the next day, 4 May, in a small committee room in the House of Lords. Before the hearing opened the Swansea Corporation made it known to the Lords Committee that they were *also* to keep a low profile; thus with the withdrawal of the Amusement Equipment Company's barrister it looked as if the SWTC were to have the proceedings completely their own way. It began to appear, indeed, that the SWTC would have no effective professional opposition to examine their evidence at all. But the SWTC

122 One of the more spectacular accidents that occasionally occurred on the route. The sign reads 'Beware of Trains'!

123 The Mumbles train could also be hired for private outings. This was taken on a private outing on a Sunday in October, 1959.

were not to have the proceedings *all* their own way; for though debarred from giving evidence themselves, the LRTL did examine the SWTC's evidence later and they published their examination in that same year. The SWTC's evidence, as given to the Lords Committee, will be considered below in the light of their results.

The plan of the committee room dictated that the Lords sat around a semi-circular table while the witnesses were required to face the Lords Committee and to address their replies and evidence to them. The chief witness for the SWTC was their General Manager, Mr H. Weedy. As the proceedings opened, Mr Weedy duly took up the required position as the

counsel for the SWTC prepared to ask him a series of carefully-prepared questions.

Counsel for the SWTC first asked Mr Weedy to confirm that the sum of £261,000 was required to finance the repair and restitution of the line and rolling stock of the Mumbles Railway. Mr Weedy confirmed that this was the case and that, moreover, his company did not have the necessary capital to undertake the task.

But what Mr Weedy did *not* explain to the Lords Committee was that the SWTC did not have that necessary capital because in 1958 they had paid in excess of £200,000 to buy the railway on which, hitherto, they had only operated the lease. It would seem, therefore, that their purchase of the railway from its two former owners had not only given the SWTC the right to determine its future, it had also deprived them of the cash reserves necessary to keep it running!

Mr Weedy was next asked whether the railway was at present making a profit. The railway, Mr Weedy announced, was not making a profit, in fact it was making a loss and had been since he joined the Company! The loss in the last full year of operation was quoted as £8,250.

But what Mr Weedy again did not explain to the Lords was that in the last year, as in all other years, even though they now owned the line, the SWTC had charged the railway with the *rental* due under the old lease. Thus the SWTC were, in effect, charging themselves rent. The rental that they charged was £13,900. This meant that, had the SWTC not charged this rent, the much-publicised *loss* of £8,250 would have been a *profit* for the undertaking of £5,500!

Mr Weedy was also asked whether, in the event of the railway's closure, the passengers would benefit directly from the substitution of motor buses for the Mumbles train. Mr Weedy assured the committee that his company proposed a massive reduction in fares for the new bus service. Indeed, with the line converted to motor buses, there would be a reduction in the price of three-monthly season tickets of as much as £2.

But in reality, a financial extrapolation of basic fares as given at the time, revealed that of the 85 basic fares, 34 would remain unchanged, 11 would be slightly reduced and 40 would be increased. It is a matter of record that this became the case. It is a further matter of record that, with the Bill safely passed, Mr Weedy's much-publicised saving of 'as much as £2' never materialised.

Many other instances of inaccuracies and inconsistencies could be cited. Mr Weedy presented inaccurate accounts of the frequency of double-track line and the number of loops that existed, this in turn giving rise to erroneous statements concerning the effici-

ency of the service. He attempted to show that the new buses would increase traffic on the Mumbles road by a mere 1%, but omitted to inform their Lordships that, for the purposes of this calculation, bicycles were assumed to be the same size as the new double-deck motor buses! It was also stated that no land existed on which the Company could construct new passing loops which would improve the train service when, in at least three places—Argyle Street, West Cross and Mumbles pier—the General Manager of the SWTC must have been aware of land, previously occupied by sidings, which could have been used for this purpose.

So why did the Amusement Equipment Company not draw the Lords attention to these inconsistencies and inaccuracies? The replacement counsel's lack of technical briefing as regards the Mumbles line must have played its part here. But even without effective professional representation and even without the active support of the Swansea Corporation, why did they not draw the Lords attention to the statements made by Mr Weedy on the financial state of the Company's accounts? According to the LRTL they could not, for the very good reason that, in direct contravention of the Companies Act, the SWTC had filed none of their accounts with the Registrar of Companies since 1956. The present day SWTC can neither confirm nor deny this charge.[5]

The Lords Committee were really in no position to do anything but pass the South Wales Transport Bill through its committee stage. Its reappearance in the Lords for its third reading came as something of a shock for those peers who had allowed it to progress beyond its second. With the dispute over the SWTC's evidence still raging, Lord Merrivale immediately recommended that an independent agent be appointed to inquire into the true facts of the matter. This advice was, however, rejected by

[5] The present day South Wales Transport Company are not the same company as that referred to here. None of the present directors or executives worked for the former SWTC and the present day company is now under the control of the National Bus Company.

Lord Merthyr who solemnly reminded the House that for over 50 years no Bill had ever been rejected by the House at its *third* reading. The Bill duly passed all its stages in the Upper House.

With the battle looking increasingly desperate, the protest movement in Swansea and Mumbles decided to make the second reading in the House of Commons the stage for their next attempt to block the passage of the Bill. A formal objection had been petitioned by three MP's, Alan Palmer, Harold Neal and Charles Hobson which stated,

> This House declines to give a second reading to a Bill against which there is strong local opposition, which seeks to replace a Railway operating on locally produced coal and on a private right of way with motor buses operating on imported fuel along congested highways and for which no valid case has been made out by the promoters of the Bill.

Prompted by this petition a debate was fixed in the House of Commons for 9 July 1959. The Minister of Transport, representing the Government's view, said that in their opinion decisions like this were best left to the operating company, i.e. to the SWTC and only *four* members spoke against the Bill. These members did draw attention to the strong local opposition to the closure, the suspect nature of the claim that the line was losing money, the folly of relying on a transport system based on imported oil rather than home produced electricity and to the tourist possibilities of the line. Further, they too advocated the appointment of an independent expert to investigate the true facts of the case.

The only MP who rose to support the Bill, Mr G. Wilson of Truro, gave as the reason for his support the 'fact' that buses do not pollute the atmosphere! If a diesel engine is properly maintained, Mr Wilson assured the House, it does not produce any smoke! But far from rejecting his argument, Mr Wilson's contribution appears to have had more effect on the Commons than the skilfully argued contribu-

tions of the four MPs who had preceded him! The Bill *passed* its second reading in the Commons with barely a murmur of dissent. Perhaps Parliament simply did not care.

Thus the battle moved on to the Commons Committee stage. The Amusement Equipment Company had, not surprisingly, now given up the fight and the only petition of substance left against the Bill was that of the Swansea Corporation, who hitherto had not had much to contribute to the fight to save the line. But finally, in July 1959, at the Commons Committee hearing, the body who many people in Swansea and Mumbles thought would be their *biggest* asset in the fight against the closure, finally made their appearance. The Swansea Corporation announced to the Commons Committee that, as a result of discussions held between themselves and the SWTC, they were now *withdrawing* all objections to that Company's plans to close the Mumbles line. The Swansea Corporation thus withdrew the *last* petition of any substance against the South Wales Transport Bill and with it came the collapse of the hopes of the protest campaign back in Swansea and the Mumbles. The only opposition now was from the National Union of Railwaymen whose sole concern was the fate of their members on the line. With the provisions they wanted inserted into the bill,[6] the South Wales Transport Bill passed on to its third reading.

With the approach of the summer recess, time was clearly becoming rather pressing for the SWTC. Mindful of this, the Company seemed to have ensured that the final stages in the passage of the Bill should have been taken at some speed, and this manipulation of the parliamentary process is not the least worrying aspect of the demise of the Mumbles Railway. In *one* day, the Bill was given a third reading, was passed back to the Lords for its

[6] The National Union of Railwaymen wished certain clauses inserted into the Bill concerning compensation of redundant staff and the transfer from rail to road services in the case of staff who were staying with SWTC. Their objections did not affect the actual passage of the Bill, merely the arrangements arising out of that passage.

118

approval of the NUR amendments, was duly approved by the Lords and two days later granted Royal Assent. Thus one day before Parliament rose for the summer recess, the South Wales Transport Bill became law.

But with the Bill on the statute book, the storm broke in Swansea and Mumbles. *Two* major issues erupted. Firstly, *why* did the barrister representing the Amusement Equipment Company quit the case so abruptly and apparently with such devastating timing the night before the committee hearing in the House of Lords? To this day, the chief witness for the Company, doesn't know and research work with the present-day company has failed

to solve the mystery. So why did the Swansea Corporation suddenly abandon *their* opposition to the closure of the Mumbles Railway at the committee stage in the House of Commons? A spokesman for the Swansea Corporation said later that the Corporation had opposed the South Wales Transport Bill at every possible stage, 'until it became obvious that the concessions of the South Wales Transport Company had deprived the Swansea Corporation of all authority and argument'. A four line report in the *South Wales Evening Post*, 8 September 1959, less than four months later completed the story,

124 An unintentionally poignant picture as events turned out! Motor buses were soon to replace the Mumbles train.

125   Notice issued by the Manager of the Mumbles Pier and Hotel after his unsuccessful attempt to prevent the closure of the Mumbles Railway.

It was announced last night by the Swansea town clerk, Mr T. B. Bowen, that when the ancient Mumbles Railway is abandoned and modern buses take its place, then all the land owned by the Railway Company—the SWTC—and additional land adjoining the Railway, is to be given free of charge by the SWTC—to the Swansea Corporation.

The fate of the Mumbles Railway was thus decided. The *manner* of that decision now matters less, of course, than its *fact*. But the questions arising out of that decision are ones that still demand answers today.

Though the fate of the railway was now decided, the residents of Swansea and Mumbles were determined that the train should not go quietly. Frustrated in their efforts to save the line, the protestors in the Mumbles decided that at least its memory should be spectacularly commemorated. The day before the last service run took place a number of Mumbles residents led by local housewife, Veronica Barrington, hired two coaches for a last private run for the people of Swansea and Mumbles. This trip was arranged to run after the last service train at 11.50 pm on 4 January 1960. As a theatrical event it was to match all the careful 150th anniversary celebrations of 1954.

The whole event was planned as a full-scale funeral procession. The residents dressed in widows' weeds and mourning clothes, they carried mourning cards, chanted funeral dirges and even had a lone trumpeter by the trackside playing 'The Last Post'. A *coffin* was carried on

126 A section of the Mumbles line closed from Southend to the Pier prior to the official closing of the whole of the Mumbles line in January 1960. Here, workmen are taking up rails to make a private road from White Gate to the Pier in the autumn of 1959.

to the train and even a ceremonial 'corpse' placed in the coffin![7] As a final touch the drivers and conductors of the railway—Frank Dunkin included—were contracted to give the train this, its most colourful, goodbye. From all over Britain applications poured in for tickets for that last trip and those who did receive tickets were to find them inscribed with a farewell rhyme,

See the train going down the track
It's sad to think it'll not come back;
It's running now for the very last time
For they are closing the oldest line.

The night of 4 January was greeted—appropriately enough—with one of the heaviest downpours the residents of Mumbles can remember. Television cameras arrived from all over the country to film the parade; their lights floodlighting the gleaming red train as the funeral party began their final procession. Each carriage was packed to capacity as the ceremonial coffin was loaded onto the front car, and to the accompaniment of hundreds of motorists tooting a cacophony of car horns,

[7] 'Ginger' Graham, Mumbles resident, with the aid of liberal quantities of alcohol!

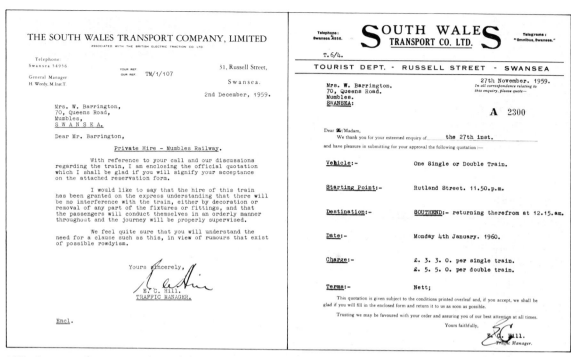

THE SOUTH WALES TRANSPORT COMPANY, LIMITED
ASSOCIATED WITH THE BRITISH ELECTRIC TRACTION CO. LTD

Telephone:
Swansea 54956

General Manager
H. Weedy, M.Inst.T.

YOUR REF.
OUR REF. TM/1/107

31, Russell Street,

Swansea.

2nd December, 1959.

Mrs. W. Barrington,
70, Queens Road,
Mumbles,
S W A N S E A.

Dear Mr. Barrington,

Private Hire - Mumbles Railway.

With reference to your call and our discussions regarding the train, I am enclosing the official quotation which I shall be glad if you will signify your acceptance on the attached reservation form.

I would like to say that the hire of this train has been granted on the express understanding that there will be no interference with the train, either by decoration or removal of any part of the fixtures or fittings, and that the passengers will conduct themselves in an orderly manner throughout and the journey will be properly supervised.

We feel quite sure that you will understand the need for a clause such as this, in view of rumours that exist of possible rowdyism.

Yours sincerely,

E. C. Hill,
TRAFFIC MANAGER.

Encl.

Telephone:
Swansea 4956

SOUTH WALE**S** TRANSPORT CO. LTD.

Telegrams:
"Omnibus, Swansea."

T.6/4.

TOURIST DEPT. - RUSSELL STREET - SWANSEA

Mrs. W. Barrington,
70, Queens Road,
Mumbles.
SWANSEA:

27th November, 1959.
In all correspondence relating to this enquiry, please quote—

A 2300

Dear Sir/Madam,

We thank you for your esteemed enquiry of ___ the 27th inst.

and have pleasure in submitting for your approval the following quotation :—

Vehicle:—	One Single or Double Train.
Starting Point:—	Rutland Street. 11.50.p.m.
Destination:—	SOUTHEND:- returning therefrom at 12.15.am.
Date:—	Monday 4th January. 1960.
Charge:—	£. 3. 3. 0. per single train. £. 5. 5. 0. per double train.
Terms:—	Nett;

This quotation is given subject to the conditions printed overleaf and, if you accept, we shall be glad if you will fill in the enclosed form and return it to us as soon as possible.

Trusting we may be favoured with your order and assuring you of our best attention at all times.

Yours faithfully,

E. C. Hill.
Traffic Manager.

127   Letter and quotation from SWTC giving details of their terms for the hire of the 'Last Wake' train. The last clause of the letter makes especially amusing reading.

the Mumbles train rocked and rolled back along the track it had travelled for 156 years.

The next day—5 January—the last service run took place. Schoolchildren left their classrooms and local people lined the streets. Pennies were put on the line to be flattened as souvenirs. The carriages were packed with invited dignitaries. It was almost as impressive a celebration as the previous night. Pictures of the procession were networked all over the world. And among the crowds and lights, the decorations and displays, enjoying the occasion as much as any of the other invited guests, were the very councillors and council officials whose actions had contributed to the closure of the line they were now so busy commemorating.

The last Mumbles train went into the Rutland Street depot at 12.20 am on 5 January 1960. 156 years of service had come to an end.

128   Mourners dressed in widow's black weep for the passing of the 156 year-old Mumbles train.

129   Mourners wait for the train at Southend.

130 The 'Wake' in full cry!

131 The ceremonial 'corpse' is loaded into the ceremonial coffin.

132 The coffin is carried by mourners towards the last train.

133   Helpers assist the Mumbles coffin onto the last Mumbles train.

134   Hundreds of people queue in the pouring rain to say goodbye to the world's oldest passenger railway.

135   The train begins its farewell journey from Southend.

136(a)   Black-edged ticket specially printed for the 'Last Wake' trip, 4 January 1960.

136(b)   Ticket for last *service* trip, 5 January 1960.

137 Last service train waits to leave the Rutland
Street terminus.

138 Foreman George prepares to open the gates for
the last service run of the Mumbles train.

139 Train No. 7 moves out of the Rutland Street
sheds ready for its trip to the Mumbles.

140   The guests arrive aboard the last service train, Deputy Mayor and Mayoress of Swansea, the Town Clerk and Mr P. Morris.

141 More guests aboard last train.

142 H. C. Drayton, Chairman of BET drives the last Mumbles train while W. T. James, Chairman of SWTC, looks on.

143 Mumbles train on its way.

144 Crowds packing the streets around the last Mumbles train.

145 Mumbles train edging its way through the crush.

146   Cars following the last service train to the Mumbles.

147 A girl puts a penny on the line to be flattened as a souvenir.

148 Last service train continues its journey.

149 Last service train nears Southend.

150   Last service train at Southend.

151 Guests and driver pose beside last service train at Southend.

152   Spectators waiting for the last train at Oystermouth.

153 Spectators waiting for the train.

154 Inspector Seacombe autographs souvenir brochures of the last Mumbles train.

155   Last service train arrives back in Rutland Street.

156 Spectators waiting to greet the train at its final destination—Rutland Street.

157 Last train returns to the Rutland Street sheds.

The South Wales Transport Co., Ltd.

A

LUNCHEON

AT THE

GUILDHALL, SWANSEA

ON THE OCCASION OF

THE CLOSING OF THE

Swansea & Mumbles Railway

5th January, 1960

THE SOUTH WALES TRANSPORT CO., LTD.

LUNCHEON

at

THE GUILDHALL, SWANSEA

on the occasion of the closing of the

SWANSEA and MUMBLES RAILWAY

TUESDAY, 5th JANUARY, 1960

GUEST LIST

Table No.		Name.		Representing.
D. 9	Abberfield	Coun. A.		
A. 20	Aldrige	J. M.		*Bus and Coach.*
A. 10	Atkin	Coun. Rev. L.		
G. 9	Bailey	H.		South Wales Transport Co., Ltd.
F. 18	Baker	D. R. S.		*Herald of Wales.*
A. 3	Ball	D. G., J.P.		Rediffusion, Ltd.
C. 11	Bartholomew	P.		T.W.W.
A. 12	Bayly	H. H.		Traffic Commissioners.
E. 11	Bellingham	R. K.		Mumbles Railway & Pier Co.
A. 19	Berry	Coun. G. C.		
F. 20	Bevan	Ald. D. F.		
D. 11	Beynon	D. W.		South Wales Transport Co., Ltd.
Top 18	Birch	R. W.		South Wales Transport Co., Ltd.
D. 4	Bishop	A. B.		Swansea Chamber of Commerce.
Top 21	Bowen	T. B., C.B.E.,		Town Clerk, Swansea.
C. 1	Brooks	W. F.		British Electric Traction Co., Ltd.
C. 10	B.B.C. Representative.			
E. 20	B.B.C. Representative.			
Top 22	Carling	A. R. F.		Public Transport Association.
E. 14	Concannon	Coun. D. C.		
B. 4	Christopher	J.		*Daily Express*
A. 8	Cross	Coun. Mrs. R., J.P.		
Top 8	Curtis	A. G., O.B.E.		Transport Commissioner for Wales and Monmouthshire.
C. 19	Daniel	Coun. M.		
G. 6	Davies	Dr. H.		
Top 26	Davies	Ifor, M.P.		
E. 3	Davies	Ald. J. G., O.B.E., J.P.		
A. 15	Davies	Coun. J. M.		

---

158 Menu for luncheon marking the closure of the Swansea and Mumbles Railway.

159 Section of guest list at closure luncheon.

160   Principal guests at closure luncheon.

161   Local dignitaries and councillors raising a cheer at the closure of the line!

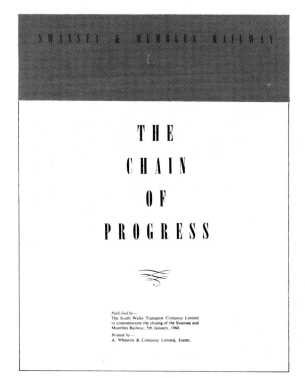

162 Front page of commemorative souvenir printed by the SWTC to mark the closure of the Swansea and Mumbles Railway.

163 Front page of booklet issued by the SWTC noting changes in service following the abandonment of the Mumbles Railway.

164   Workmen taking up the rails of the Mumbles line, March 1960.

IN MEMORIAM

THE BALLAD OF THE LAVARBREAD EXPRESS[8]   *Ivor Owen Morgan*

The Beetle Squasher—you know it, boys,
It crawls along with a rattling noise,
With a clatter just like German toys,
   On the Mumbles Railway!

   Chorus—
      Rattle clatter all the way,
      Rattle clatter all the way,
      Rattle clatter all the way,
         Along the Mumbles Railway!

The Swansea Boys, you must confess,
Love the Lavarbread Express,
The engine they would all caress
   On the Mumbles Railway!

From Rutland Street to Pier it goes,
When we'll get there no-one knows,
We start in summer and end in snows,
   On the Mumbles Railway!

The engine! Oh it is a scream!
More a nightmare than a dream!
It belches ashes, soot and steam
   On the Mumbles Railway!

Before the train has time to start,
It stops again and some depart,
It's quicker far by farmer's cart
   Than by the Mumbles Railway!

On the engine is a bell,
Ting-a-ling, a ding-dong bell,
If you're squashed you won't look well
   On the Mumbles Railway!

A snail dashed past us one fine day,
Our startled driver passed away
And Major Segrave stood at bay,
   On the Mumbles Railway!

We're on the train, we heave a sigh!
Puff! Puff!—and the ashes fly!
You dig the grit out of your eye
   On the Mumbles Railway!

We slip apass the Slip, and so
On to Brynmill! Tally ho!
On to Blackpill, crawling slow
   On the Mumbles Railway!

Ha'penny or a penny, O!
Shout the boys and cartwheels throw!
You fling them coins as on you go
   On the Mumbles Railway!

At last we steam into West Cross;
A trusty steed—our iron hoss!
Dead on time—just ask the 'Boss'
   On the Mumbles Railway!

Away we crawl to Oystermouth,
Stop at Southend, further south,
An engine foaming at the mouth,
   On the Mumbles Railway!

The Pier we reach—our troubles past!
We have a shave, and break our fast!
And look amazed, and stand aghast
   On the Mumbles Railway!

*   *   *

In Nineteen Hundred and Twenty-Nine,
Magician's wand—the Mumbles line—
Electric trains, all fast and fine
   On the Mumbles Railway!

Travelling smoothly all the way,
Travelling smoothly all the way,
Travelling smoothly all the way,
   Toot, toot! Mumbles Railway!

In One Nine Six and add a nought,
The Mumbles Train—a dreadful thought—
Will stop for good—it didn't ought —
   No more Mumbles Railway!

[8] This ballad can be sung to the tune of 'The Great American Railway'.

Chapter 9

THE REVIVAL OF THE MUMBLES RAILWAY?

A new Mumbles Railway! That's the dream of the Mumbles Railway Society who say that the Railway could be re-established in a form which will not be detrimental to existing facilities along the Swansea Bay. The Society's Management Committee who are finalising proposals for a new line say that these are not 'pie in the sky' plans and they are to launch a publicity campaign in January.

(Evening Post, 15/12/75)

The end of the story for the ancient Mumbles Railway? Not quite. The *revival* of its story was prompted by a simple advertisement that appeared in the national press in August 1975,

Hallmark Replicas Limited, London, proudly offer for sale gold-plated reproductions of the Post Office stamps to commemorate the world's *first* public Railway which came into being at Stockton and Darlington 150 years ago in 1825.

For many people in Swansea this advertisement was the straw that broke the camel's back. Over the fifteen years that had elapsed since the closure of the railway, Swansea had witnessed a succession of humiliations with respect to its most famous historical asset. The Swansea Museum had expressed no interest in keeping any of the electric railway's coaches or engines at the time of the closure of the line in 1960 even though *22* other museums throughout Britain had requested items from the old line. 'There is nothing characteristic about it,'[1] said Dr Percy Little, Curator of the Swansea Museum. It is

165 Demolition of the Mumbles Railway.

[1] Quoted in the *Evening Post*, 5/1/60.

fortunate that other organisations disagreed with Dr Little's assessment, most particularly the Middleton Railway Preservation Society, Leeds. This Society, led by its Chairman, Dr R. F. Youell, led a campaign in the spring of 1960 to save the last surviving Mumbles Railway coach. The success of his venture was reported in a long and evocative letter by Dr Youell published in the *Evening Post* later that year,

> Mumbles train number 2 now rests safe and sound in a siding on the Middleton Railway at Leeds after the most varied fortnight in her 30 year career.
>
> Number 2 left Swansea East Goods Yard by the 8.27 am train on the 13 June. Two members of the Middleton Railway Preservation Society were allowed to travel in the brake van by British Railways throughout the journey to photograph the Mumbles train's farewell to Wales.
>
> For three miles Number 2 travelled alongside Swansea Bay within feet of the partly dismantled tracks that she had so many times traversed. Then across Mumbles road she swung inland and turned north for her 225 mile trip to Leeds.

A

SHERRY EVENING

will be held in aid of the Preservation of the

MUMBLES RAILWAY TRAIN

and its journey to the 1758 Middleton Railway, Leeds

AT PENGROES, MUMBLES ROAD, WEST CROSS

ON WEDNESDAY 27th JULY 1960 7 - 9 p m

TICKETS 2/-

166 Ticket for Sherry Evening organised by Veronica Barrington to raise funds for the rescue of the Mumbles electric train No. 2 by the Middleton Railway Preservation Society, Leeds.

The train ambled along at a steady pace, shunting now and again to avoid expresses or to pick up extra wagons. At every Welsh stopping place, crowds gathered to see the Mumbles train on its three bogie wagons. At Llandovery, railwaymen chalked 'Cymru am Byth' on the lower deck as a farewell gesture. Handbills were distributed to all the interested spectators telling the story of the Mumbles train's journey.

At Knighton Wales was left behind. Running down to Shrewsbury from Church Stretton, the 50 mph mark was reached— good going for an ordinary goods train. By Monday evening we reached Crewe sorting sidings for a six-hour break.

Remarshalled in a new train, the Mumbles train left at dawn on Tuesday the 14th for Stockport and Huddersfield. More shunting took place, this time into a train for Copley Hill depot at Leeds. Finally a special trip was made to take the three special wagons to Balm Road, the junction for the Middleton Railway, arriving at 3.30 pm.

British Railways officials turned out as helpful at Leeds as they had been at Swansea. After a local firm had lent their crane for off-loading the bogies and a gang of students had jacked the bottom deck into place, a special journey was made across the London to Glasgow main line to get the Mumbles train on to the Middleton Railway.

Because the Mumbles train would not couple up to British Railways stock, special towing tackle had to be employed using wire ropes. Everything went without a hitch and hauled by the Middleton Railway's own locomotive (the first diesel engine made in Leeds in 1932) the Mumbles train entered the Middleton Railway, the first passenger train to run in its 202-year existence.

The top deck was lifted from a convenient railway bridge and the lower deck was

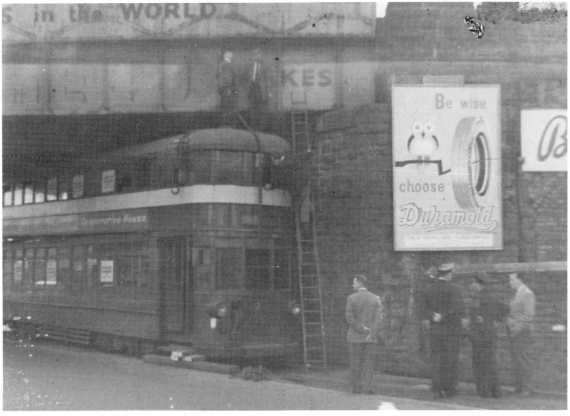

167   Dismantling of train Number 2 begins in preparation for its trip to Leeds.

shunted beneath it. Then the 'lower away' signal was given and the two halves fitted together perfectly. An army of workers then descended on the train screwing back the scores of bolts holding the two halves together.

The pantograph current collector was fixed on top, the seats and door mechanism were put back and in less than three days the re-assembly was complete. A vigorous wash-down and window polish made the train ready for her first public appearance in Leeds.

Apart from the window broken during

shunting at Huddersfield the train has not sustained so much as a scratch since leaving Swansea.

Showing Swansea at one end, Mumbles pier at the other end and Oystermouth at the sides, with all the Swansea advertisements still in place, Number 2 ran for a whole week to raise funds for Leeds University Charity Rag Week. Over 7,500 passengers were given rides in this week and a substantial sum was given to local charities.

A local firm of gas engineers allowed the Middleton Railway Preservation Society to use their part of the Middleton Railway for

168　Top half of Mumbles electric train separated from bottom, ready to be winched onto lowloaders.

the occasion and have stored the Mumbles train in their yard until a permanent depot can be built for her. Day after day, the crowds turned up to watch the unique spectacle—the world's oldest railway, the last survivor from the world's first passenger railway and the first diesel locomotive built in Leeds (itself a major locomotive building city).

On the first day a special trip was made for the first passenger who was Mrs Langton of Bramley, Leeds, whose parents came from

Briton Ferry. Her husband worked on the Mumbles Railway. She has been in Leeds for 25 years and is now an old age pensioner. A surprisingly large number of people turned up or sent messages of congratulation during the week.

So train Number 2, restored in her siding, is spick and span as if she had just come out of the Rutland Street depot. We have an historic consignment note from British Railways asking the Middleton Railway to accept one train in three wagon loads consigned from

169   Bottom half of Mumbles train outside Swansea Museum which refused to house it. The train is ready for its trip to Leeds.

the Swansea and Mumbles Railway. This is probably the first time BR have been employed by two railways older than themselves. The cost of the journey worked out at less than one half that by road to Leeds.

One thing we did not clean off when washing down was the 'Cymru am Byth' chalked on the sides. It seemed somehow sacrilege to wipe it off. So this farewell message from Wales will stay there until rain or a repaint efface it. Even then we shall still look upon the Mumbles train as 28½ tons of Wales in our midst as she takes her place as the showpiece of the Middleton Railway.

Susan Youell in her article 'The Third Century at Middleton'[2] confirms that the Mumbles train was running 'completely reassembled in Leeds within ten days'. As recognition of their efforts, the SWTC donated two of the remaining signals from the old Mumbles Railway to the Middleton Railway Preservation Society to be kept in Leeds. That the Society deserved their gift was undeniable. But, as the *Evening Post* somewhat sadly pointed out,

[2] Susan M. Youell, 'The Third Century at Middleton: A Short History of the Middleton Colliery Railway Leeds and its Revival Under the Middleton Railway Preservation Society', *Railway Magazine*, April 1961.

So another relic leaves the town which made history by having the oldest passenger railway in the world. Little now remains to remind people of that fact.[3]

But at least the relics had been *saved*. The same could not be said of the only surviving engine, 'Tirdonkin', from the train's steam era. This had been scrapped only days before another preservation society could reach it. The track bed on which the train ran had been left to decay during the 1960s and at the end of the decade had become partly covered by a tip. Worse, however, was to follow. In 1967 the surviving Mumbles electric coach on the Middleton Railway was attacked by vandals and its windows were broken, its doors smashed and its seats cut to ribbons. Three years later, in 1970, the final nail was hammered in the coffin when the coach was completely destroyed by fire. Dr Youell's efforts had, ten years later, come to nothing.

The decay continued throughout the 1970s. The old Rutland Street terminus, site of the oldest passenger booking office in the world, was demolished to make way for road improvements, and the only remaining relic from the old train itself left in Swansea—the front cab of electric train Number 7—had been left exposed to the elements for so long that there were fears it had rusted beyond repair. This litany of neglect was compounded by the appearance of advertisements such as that celebrating the Stockton and Darlington Railway as the world's *first* public line. It seemed as if Swansea was doomed to suffer further humiliation at the hands of other railways claiming that which rightfully belonged to the Mumbles Railway. Fortunately there were people in Swansea who decided it was time to call a halt.

In 1975 the Mumbles Railway Society was formed. Its founders were: Chairman, Tony Cottle, Hon. Secretary, Ron Lawson, Hon. Treasurer, John Pile, with Leslie Evans, John Llewellyn, Christopher Morton, Peter Trem-

170 The only surviving major relic of the Mumbles train in Swansea; the front cab of train Number 7, the train that ran the last service trip on 5 January 1960.

ewan and Gaynor Tremewan. Initially it was established to counteract the past neglect of the line and the growing ignorance about its importance by staging exhibitions and arranging lectures, talks and slide shows illustrating the railway's history. The exhibitions have since included actual items from the train's past including a small section of the original horse-drawn track and two flintlock hand pistols, thought also to date back to the very first horse-drawn passenger journey, as well as the more usual collection of photographs and

[3] *Evening Post*, 4/9/61.

158

postcards of the old railway. One such exhibition took place at Ashley's Restaurant, Mumbles, on 25 March 1977 to celebrate the 170th anniversary of the inauguration of the passenger service on the line. The extent of local interest was indicated by the fact that over 1,500 people visited the display and at the end of the day many hundreds of others had to be turned away by the Society's organisers.

However, the activities of the Society were not confined solely to recollections of the railway's history. The actual *revival* of a section of the line was also a prime objective and the Society soon began an aggressive and well-publicised campaign to this end. Its objectives were made clear in the Society's first Newsletter, published in 1976 under the auspices of its Management Committee:

171 Train Number 7, the only surviving cab, outside St Helen's.

What we are proposing is a 2 ft gauge railway modelled on the very successful 'Great Little Trains of Wales'. Motive power would be provided by small steam locomotives, oil-fired for cleanliness and requiring no facilities for coal storage and ash disposal. Though originally designed to work in the slate quarries, many of these fascinating little engines have been rebuilt and 'promoted' to hauling passenger trains on the thriving narrow-gauge railways of the Principality. The kitchen maid has become a star. 'Pixie' is a good example of the type of locomotive we would like to see puffing along the new Mumbles Railway to revive a part of Swansea's heritage of nearly 170 years. Though much smaller than the original pannier tanks which worked on the line—she is only 8 ft high and 10 ft long—'Pixie' is capable of hauling up to 100 passengers. This engine worked in the Northamptonshire iron-ore mines for many years but is now owned by the Rev. Teddy Boston and runs on the Cadby Railway in the grounds of the rectory. She was built in 1919.

Originally it was proposed that the restored railway would run from St Helen's to Oystermouth Square. It would use the old Mumbles Railway track bed from Blackpill to Oystermouth and the old LMS track bed from Blackpill to St Helen's. The Mumbles Railway Society backed their Newsletter with a special brochure entitled *Bring Back the Mumbles Train*, stressing that,

This 4-mile journey would offer the people of Swansea and visitors to the city an unrivalled opportunity of viewing this magnificent Bay and of going back for a while to the great age of steam. A live steam railway of such historic importance would be of considerable publicity value to the Swansea area.

Interest in the area began to be aroused. The Society next arranged a meeting between themselves and the Swansea City Council's

Policy and Resources Committee in the early part of 1976, although they made one change to their well-publicised policy prior to the meeting to enhance the chances of their proposals being accepted. The Society decided that the line should not run from St Helen's to Oystermouth, but should follow the shorter route from Blackpill to Oystermouth. The amended route would thus follow the old Mumbles Railway route along the whole of its length. The proposals that were submitted to Swansea City Council read as follows,

A narrow-gauge railway operating between Blackpill and Oystermouth would be a viable unit similar to the 2 mile Llanberis Lake Railway in North Wales. Your committee ruled out from the beginning any question of going beyond Oystermouth to the pier because of the extensive use being made of this section by the sailing boats which add so much charm and interest to Mumbles.

By contrast the foreshore between Blackpill and Oystermouth has few demands made upon it. Access to the beach would not be cut off by the kind of railway we envisage and the leisurely passage of a small-scale train at hourly intervals during the summer is unlikely to disturb the composure of any angler.

Blackpill is the obvious starting point for the construction of the new Mumbles Railway. There is an existing recreational complex to which the railway could be regarded as an additional attraction and there is space

172   Train Number 7 at West Cross.

for the modest facilities needed to operate the line. These amount to nothing more than the equivalent of a small petrol filling station.

A length of about 100 yards from Blackpill to Lilliput Lane is the first stage of track-laying planned and with volunteer labour this could be completed in about ten weekends. Out-and-back rides should be available as construction continued in stages via West Cross to the final terminus near Oystermouth Square. As with the old steam trains the complete journey from Blackpill to Oystermouth would take 18 minutes at a speed of about 7 mph giving passengers time to enjoy the unrivalled scenic attractions of Swansea Bay and Mumbles.

In the long term it would be a fairly simple matter to bridge the small stream at Blackpill for such lightweight locomotives and extend the line to St Helen's or even perhaps to the new Leisure Centre following the old LMS route. The selective development of tourism means more jobs for Swansea people without damaging the environment and the new Mumbles Railway is a forward-looking project. Our aim is to use the best features of the past to create something of great benefit for the future.

The Society drew attention to the large public interest their proposals had aroused and backed their proposals with a feasibility study undertaken by the civil engineering firm of W. S. Atkins and Partners who confirmed that

173   Train Number 7 at Norton Road.

the laying and operating of a narrow-gauge railway between Blackpill and Oystermouth was a feasible and practical possibility. The engineers did recommend that the route should be placed on the *seaward* side of the existing footpath which would involve the least interference with pedestrian traffic and would also provide attractive opportunities for landscaping the areas around Blackpill. Their report also took account of the important issue of safety and recommended that, although the speed of the proposed train would be limited to 7 mph, a,

> . . . low simple fence is erected between the footpath and the railway route to provide a physical separation between the train and pedestrians. Warning signs should also be erected at each access point to the beach to warn pedestrians and to instruct the engine driver to take extra care and to sound the engine whistle.

The Mumbles Railway Society duly met the City of Swansea's Policy and Resources Committee in the first week of February, 1976, but it was to prove a frustrating affair. The Policy and Resources Committee opposed the proposed development largely, so it seems, on the specific issue of the *fencing*. The Director of Environment claimed that the proposed fence would prevent access to the seafront, an objection supported by the Gower Society who released a statement claiming that, if the line was authorised, the Department of the Environment would insist on fencing on either side of the track which would 'greatly detract from the landscaping already carried out by the Swansea City Council and would impede free access to the seafront'. Thus, for the present, the development was blocked.

But the issue of fencing was also to prove a bone of contention amongst the ranks of the Mumbles Railway Society. One of its members, the Hon. Secretary, Ron Lawson, had already voiced his reservations about the desirability of the fencing requirements attendant on the proposed steam-operated service. Contemporary traffic requirements stated that any steam-operated line of more than 15″ gauge must be fenced along the whole of its length to a minimum height of 3 ft, and Mr Lawson felt that this would be environmentally

174   Advertisement for 170th anniversary party held in Ashley's Restaurant, Mumbles, on 25 March 1977.

unacceptable along the Mumbles foreshore. Unable to reach agreement with the other members of the Society on changing the method of traction, Mr Lawson resigned his position as Honorary Secretary in November 1976 and formed a rival organisation, the Mumbles Railway Company Limited. This undertaking was registered as a private company with much the same intentions as the original Mumbles Railway Society, but with different proposals on how to achieve those aims.

The Mumbles Railway Company Limited initially proposed to revive the Mumbles Railway by laying a length of unfenced tramway between Blackpill and Oystermouth, flush to the ground, and operated by *horse-drawn* cars, thus reverting to the original type of motive power used in the early nineteenth century. However, a commissioned independent feasibility study prepared by a firm of railway construction experts appears to have led to a change in the Company's proposals. The new proposals were set out in a document based on that feasibility study and entitled 'A New Role for the Mumbles Railway':

Given the right kind of restoration, the Mumbles Railway could be re-opened from Blackpill to Oystermouth without any detriment whatsoever to the amenities. There are special environmental factors which have to be taken into account on this 1¾ mile stretch of the foreshore, but they can all be fully satisfied by narrow-gauge *battery-operated trams*.

Travelling at a maximum speed of 8 mph, these vehicles are safe and clean. They do not need overhead wires or continuous fencing of the track. What is more, trams bear a marked resemblance to the red electric cars most people will remember with affection as the 'Mumbles train'. The photograph shows the grass verge running from Blackpill towards Oystermouth on which a tramway could be laid quite unobtrusively with no effect on the path and no restriction on access to the sands.

The project would benefit the people of Swansea without making any call on the rates because, like the original Mumbles Railway, it can be financed on a commercial basis. The approval and goodwill of the City Council, as owners of the land, are of course essential. However it is the policy of the Council to promote Swansea, Mumbles and Gower as a tourist area and nothing could further this policy more than to have an electric tramway, unique in Wales, operating at Blackpill.

Earlier this year local public opinion was shown to be very much in favour of restoring a part of the Mumbles Railway. A recent feasibility study by a well-known firm of consulting engineers undertaken for the M.R.S. has confirmed that a narrow-gauge line between Blackpill and Oystermouth Bus Station is practicable. Such facilities as car parks and conveniences already exist at the proposed termini.

The electricity sub-station at Blackpill was designed for the Mumbles Railway by the Borough Architect, Mr Ernest Morgan ARIBA and completed in 1927 . . . The Mumbles train could again run from here taking 15 minutes to reach Oystermouth over what is still the most attractive part of its former route. By arrangement with the City Council, the small sub-station building (now a store) might be used as a booking office and small tramway museum. As the first place in Wales to have electric trams, Swansea is not an inappropriate location, further historical interest being added by the Constitution Hill tramway 1896-1903. This was cable-hauled like the San Francisco Trams which, significantly, are seen so often on TV and in American airline advertising.

The Mumbles Railway Company also proposed a secondary scheme which Mr Lawson had attempted to introduce into the Mumbles Railway Society's original proposals in 1975, but which was not considered appropriate at that time by other members of the Management Committee. This proposed a second narrow-gauge railway, operated by steam, which would be constructed along the Clyne valley on the old LMS track bed. The opening paragraphs of the Mumbles Railway Company's second report, 'Steam in the Clyne valley', summarises this proposal,

Across the road from the Mumbles Railway at Blackpill there was an LMS station on the former main line from Swansea (Victoria) to Shrewsbury and Crewe, via Central Wales. Originally opened through the Clyne valley in 1867 as the 'Llanelly Railway' . . . the establishment of a tramway between Blackpill and Oystermouth would build up sufficient demand to justify laying a narrow-gauge railway to be worked by steam. The two systems could be connected for passengers by means of a footbridge at Blackpill.

A narrow-gauge railway into the Clyne valley from Blackpill would open up picnic sites which are otherwise inaccessible, relieving some of the pressure on the existing picnic areas in Gower at peak periods. And there is at least one possible location for a summer adventure centre in the valley.

Expanding a new Mumbles Railway system from Blackpill towards Gowerton has the immense advantage in the long term of taking a railway closer to the M.4 motorway so that a proportion of the traffic visiting the system could be accommodated at some point between Gowerton and Dunvant. A tourist centre here would be the ideal terminus for the narrow-gauge line from Blackpill.

Huge capital outlay is not necessary to get this project going. A start can be made simply by laying the first ½ mile of tramway (i.e. the proposed line from Blackpill to Oystermouth as the essential first stage) and operating it as a temporary measure with a single horse-drawn car.

Thus two alternative schemes were now on the table. Pressed by both organisations, the Swansea City Council on 31 March 1977 once again agreed that their Policy and Resources Committee should meet both railway organisations for discussions of their respective plans. The meeting would also investigate the possibility of an alternative railway track placed in the Clyne valley. Again the Mumbles Railway Society and the Mumbles Railway Company embarked on a sustained campaign of lobbying and pressurising individual councillors but later that year a report of the Policy

175 Restoration work begins on the front cab of train Number 7.

and Resources Committee rejected *both* schemes. Again the Committee raised the issue of fencing which they believed would be environmentally undesirable,[4] called into question the economics of undertaking such a scheme and also drew attention to the lack of car parking facilities at either end of the proposed line. The last word was left to Council-

[4] The Policy and Resources Committee seem to have completely ignored the points made by Mr Lawson in his deposition.

lor Reg Crimp who declared that if either scheme went ahead it would result in the 'environmental vandalism' of the seafront.

Interest in the restoration of the railway has not, however, died. The 175th anniversary of the establishment of the passenger service, celebrated in 1982, saw an impressive pageant of activities which testify to a deep and continuing interest in the Mumbles Railway.

British Rail named a new locomotive, 'Oystermouth', in honour of its earliest fore-

176 Front cab of train number 7, clearly rotted and rusted is winched from the Museum grounds to be restored.

bear. The Church of Wales gave permission for a new stained-glass window to be installed in the Parish Church of All Saints, Oystermouth, dedicated to St Christopher, the patron saint of travellers and depicting all three periods in the life of the Oystermouth train. The electric car that was left rotting in the grounds of the Maritime Museum became the subject of an intensive restoration exercise undertaken by the Museum staff and was duly restored to its former glory and is now on permanent display in Swansea's Maritime Museum. Lord Parry, Chairman of the Wales Tourist Board, presided over a celebration luncheon held in the Guildhall in honour of the anniversary; and the Post Office, previously obdurate in its refusal to commemorate the line, issued a special first-day cover in recognition of the line's historic antecedents. Countless displays, exhibitions and meetings also took place along the length of Swansea Bay to mark the railway's anniversary.

177   Inspection of the front cab of train Number 7 begins.

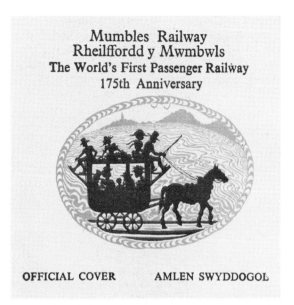

Mumbles Railway
Rheilffordd y Mwmbwls
The World's First Passenger Railway
175th Anniversary

OFFICIAL COVER   AMLEN SWYDDOGOL

178 Lord and Lady Mayoress of Swansea hand-stamp the official first day cover commemorating the 175th anniversary of the Mumbles Railway, celebrated on 25 March 1982. The first cover was sent to Her Majesty the Queen.

179 Official first day cover commemorating the 175th anniversary of the Mumbles Railway.

180 Lord and Lady Mayoress of Swansea pose beside British Rail's new train, 'Oystermouth', named in honour of its earliest forebear.

THE MUMBLES RAILWAY SOCIETY

requests the pleasure of your company at the

DEDICATION AND UNVEILING OF THE ST. CHRISTOPHER WINDOW

to mark the 175th Anniversary of the
World's First Passenger Railway

at All Saints' Church, Oystermouth

on Thursday, 25th March, 1982, at 11 a.m.

R.S.V.P. to
Mrs. V. Barrington,
81, Mumbles Road,
West Cross,
Swansea, SA3 5AA.

181   Invitation to attend unveiling of stained glass window in Oystermouth Church to mark the 175th anniversary of the world's first railway.

182   The unveiling of the stained glass window in Oystermouth Church, 25 March 1982.

The Bone Shaker

The Mumbles Railway Cocktail

```
VODKA

DUBONNET

GRENADINE

ORANGE SQUASH

DASH OF ANGOSTURA BITTERS


Strained into a Hi-Ball glass
Topped with Tonic Water


*


Especially created by Richard,
Chairman of the South Wales Area of
The United Kingdom Bartenders Guild


*


THURSDAY 25th.MARCH 1982
```

183   Recipe for special Mumbles Railway cocktail. Guaranteed to shake more than your bones!

CITY OF SWANSEA

The pleasure of your company is requested

at the opening of the Exhibition

to celebrate the 175th anniversary

of the world's first passenger railway

'The Mumbles Railway'

by

The Right Worshipful The Lord Mayor of Swansea
Councillor Paul Valerio

at the Maritime & Industrial Museum
South Dock, Swansea.

at 7.00 p.m. on Thursday 25th March, 1982

Admit Two   R.S.V.P.

184   Invitation to attend the permanent exhibition opened at Swansea's Industrial and Maritime Museum on the occasion of the 175th anniversary of the establishment of the passenger service on the line. The front cab of train Number 7, fully restored, is on permanent exhibition in the Museum.

THE MUMBLES RAILWAY DINNER 1982

In the Mumbles Railway Restaurant at the Bay View Hotel, 400 Oystermouth Road, Swansea

Wednesday, September 29th

7.30 for 8.00 p.m.

Lounge suits

185   Countless dinners and social occasions marked the railway's 175th anniversary, including the above at the newly-opened Mumbles Railway Restaurant in the Bay View Hotel, Swansea.

186   Interior of Mumbles Railway Restaurant with its decorations completely given over to pictures and memorabilia of the old Mumbles train.

So where is the end of the story for the Mumbles Railway? *Is* there an end? It is as well to remember that the railway closed once before, for a 33 year period between 1827 and 1860. Is it possible, as increasing numbers of people now hope, that the present will prove, again, a temporary pause? Could a *second* revival of the Mumbles train be a real possibility? Could the Mumbles train be running again along the Mumbles foreshore within the next few years? This book ends, firmly and unequivocally, with that hope.

SELECTED BIBLIOGRAPHY

Swansea Improvements and Tramways Company, *Swansea and Mumbles Railway 1804-1904 Centenary Souvenir*, June 29 and 30, 1904, Swansea, Watkins, 1904.

South Wales Transport Company, *Electrification of the Mumbles Railway 1928*, Swansea Printers, 1928.

South Wales Transport Company, *The Oldest Passenger Railway in the World*, SWTC, 1954.

South Wales Transport Company, *Swansea and Mumbles Railway: The Chain of Progress*, SWTC, 1960.

'The Oldest Railway in the World', *Railway Magazine*, July, 1908.

Charles E. Lee, *The First Passenger Railway*, Oakwood Press, South Godstone, Surrey, 1942, reprinted as *The Swansea and Mumbles Railway*, 1954, reprinted 1977.

Norman L. Thomas, *The Mumbles: Past and Present*, UBS, Swansea, 1978.

G. B. Claydon, 'Swansea Swan Song', *Modern Tramway*, Vol. 22, No. 262, October 1959.

Susan M. Youell, 'The Third Century at Middleton: A Short History of the Middleton Colliery Railway, Leeds and its Revival under the Middleton Railway Preservation Society'. *Railway Magazine*, April 1961.

H. Libby, *The Mixture: Mumbles and Harry Libby*, 1964.

The Mumbles Train: A Collection of Newspaper Cuttings on the Mumbles train from the *Evening Post* between 1952 and 1967, Swansea Central Reference Library.

Ron Lawson, *A New Role for the Mumbles Railway*, 1976.

Mumbles Railway Society, *The Mumbles Railway: The World's First Passenger Railway*, MRS, 1981.

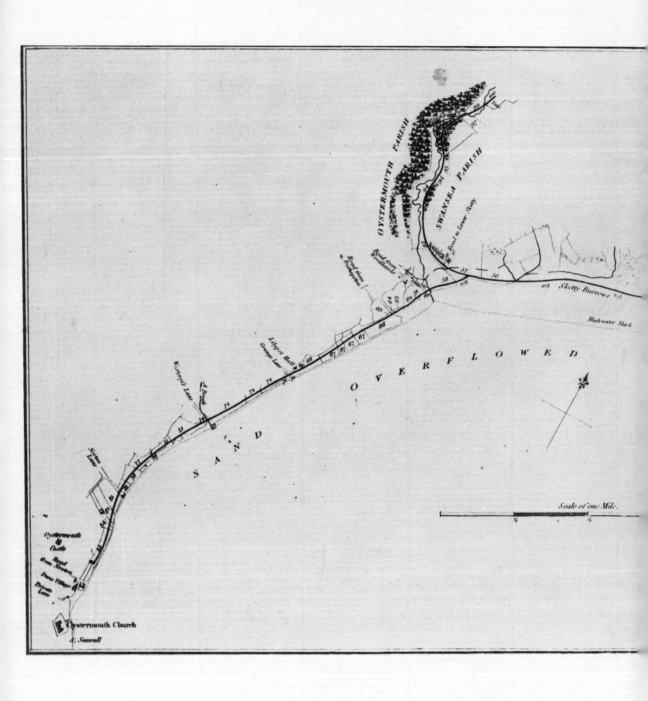

OYSTERMOUTH PARISH

SWANSEA PARISH

Road to Lower Sketty

Road from Woodlands

Road from Blackpames

Sketty Burrows

Highwater Mark

SAND   OVERFLOWED

Lilliput Hall

George Lane

Newbridge Lane

Clyne

Scale of one Mile.

Oystermouth
Castle

Road from
Newton

Dunns Village

Private Lane

Oystermouth Church

A Seawall